*"No-one and everyone
must repeatedly
re-engage and merge."*

Globlquest Publishing
globalquest28@gmail.com

© Keith Simons 2022
www.spiritual-narratives.net

This book is copyright. Apart from any fair dealing for the purposes of private study, research or review permitted under the Copyright Act 1968, no part may be stored or reproduced by any process without prior written permission. Enquiries should be made to the publisher.

Simons, Keith, 1949-2022,
Merged Voices/Keith Simons.
ISBN 978-0-9758365-6-9
1. Simons, Keith, 1949-2022.

A catalogue record for this book is available from the National Library of Australia

MERGED VOICES

A SOUL CLUSTER COLLABORATION

BINDO,
KRISHNAJI,
DAVID,
MASSIMO,
ALEKSANDR

AND

KEITH

"Hold to the sacred center. This is the great transformation happening before your eyes."

CONTENTS

Introduction: From the Collaborators 9
Foreward 11
Elucia - How to be receptive to the spiritual realms 13

AN OPENING CONVERSATION

Bindo 17
Krishnaji 22
David 28
Krishnaji 2 30
Keith 32
Parelsitis 36

MERGED VOICES: *A Soul Cluster Collaboration*

Life, Death and Freedom 39
Complexity and Contextuality 42
Conspiracy, Lies and Deception 45
Transparent Collaboration 49
Inner Collaborative Transparency 51
The Battle between Two Forces 54

continued ..

CONTENTS *(continued)*

MERGED VOICES: *A Soul Cluster Collaboration*

Imitation 57
Awakening to Reality 59
The Challenge... 62
Walking the Talk.. 65
Motivation 68
Substances and Human Potential.. 69
Incrementalism and Gradualism... 72
Taking a Plunge 74
The Great Threshold... 77
The Adversary 80
Microcosmic Dramas.. 84
Meditation and Mindfulness... 87
Deconstruction and Cover Stories 88
Metaphorical Eruptions 90
The Witness 93
Alchemy of Transformation 95

CONTENTS *(continued)*

MERGED VOICES: *Across the Threshhold*

Massimo - Crossing the Threshold into an Awakening of the Consciousness Soul or I Am 99
How to Awaken the Spiritually Sleeping? 101
Soul Cluster (Group Mind) 103
Immediacy 105
Aleksandr 107
Moral Choices 109
Entrapment 112
Beyond Entrapment 119

AFTERWORD

My Own Freedom Story 131
Conversations with the Cabal 133

Introduction

from the collaborators ...

It has been decided and decoded following the inter-dimensional transmissions from Elucia and Parelsitus that we of your related discarnate soul clusters should contribute from our own connected perspectives. The varied soul missions and evolutional developments of those who belong to resonant soul-clusters add to the larger picture by sharing and building on each other's understandings and use of language.

Working with the largest multi-dimensional perspectives has been a mission for millennia. Incarnationally this has manifested as artist, revolutionary, activist, scientist, writer and spiritual leader, all interweaving and expressing in myriads of ways, attempting to make an impact within the evolutionary processes of our beloved planet.

We have worked with the author before. This has now reached a further stage of necessity, as a need to explain subtleties that haven't been shared by our co-workers in this worthy experiment that has been taken on, invited us to participate in, and, with some help from other incarnated souls, will bring to the attention of many and join with the radical wave and downpouring of higher spiritual energies.

This is a threshold phase for our universe to recalibrate, redesign, reactivate and positively mutate into a transformed way of being, awakened consciousness and cooperative ventures that are globally responsible and spiritualised trans-dimensional experiences.

Revelation will be your heart opening! Your heart eyes will experience revelation! "

Foreward

It is the threshhold of another year, going from 2022 into 2023. My husband Keith Simons, crossed the threshhold of death in full consciousness on the 9th February 2022, after a short illness. This book contains some of his final works, written in communication with discarnate souls that he was and remains connected with. Usually it began with him connecting with them by reading their books, writtten in their last incarnation. Keith read extensively and widely. He had a great capacity to take in many and vast ideas, philosophies and spiritual works. Then, through a type of meditative inquiry, he could make a connection with their soul in the discarnate realm, communicate with them and bring their responses through into written form.

These particular communications started about fifteen years ago, the first series are documented in the book 'Portal: Awakening to Being'. They soon metamorphosed into a 'merged' form, where the individual voice was subsumed into the collective voice. Sometimes though, the individual soul's orientation, particular interest, expertise in a past incarnation and preparation for a future incarnation become recognisable. Elucia had been a significant soul, as had Paralsitus. Their transmissions are contained in whole books. It shouldn't be too difficult to work out who they were in their most recent incarnations. But they did not wish to have an emphasis on this. They had had many signficant incarnations, and more to come, as part of the 'Great Work'. Keith, too, could recall at least three significant incarnations, and therefore karmic relationships with some of the discarnate ones. One of these was referred to at times in the writing. Again, he never put any emphasis on this, instead he accepted that his would be a humble, and largely unrecognised life where he could develop his spiritual capacities, address his wayward tendencies, and continue to develop his passion for truth, love, poetry and the Word.

When these transmissions began, Keith would speak them, and I would write them into notebooks. After a time, Keith could inwardly listen to the communication and write it without having me as an intermediary. Always, he would pause, empty himself, perhaps allow a question to form, and then 'receive' the response and set himself to writing. He practised doing this with others, via a written text, a real person, a discarnate soul, or a group of souls. Some of these books have been published, some are yet to be published.

I will leave you with the advice of the soul we named 'Elucia', who helped us to understand how to refine the work by developing our inner life. In this way Keith could become a better conduit for the wisdom that would downflow into his creative outpourings. Just before he died, he challenged himself to get to know the adversary better — Ahriman and the Cabal were in conversation with him. Some of this was very intense and challenging, and did not make it through into written form. There is a fragment at the end of this book, to give you a taste.

Leanne Simons, December 2022

How to be receptive to the spiritual realms

The soul is to be considered as the intermediary between the spiritual realms and the physical-sensory realms. The soul is not a mental construction. The soul is extraordinarily sensitive. I can only reach you through the sensitivity of your soul. To be really receptive to me, you have to really surrender to the sensitivity of your soul. Because of the relative grossness of the sensory world you inhabit, it can feel very difficult, even unlikely, to be able to receive me. It is this experiential shift from the experience of the gross-sensual to the subtlety of the soul-sensitive, open receptivity that constitutes an essential aspect of the spiritual life. Without being able to—actually be able to shift experience this way, spiritual work remains just pure theory. If people cannot actually receive me, but only relate to me through words written in books, then they are missing crucial understanding. If someone can receive me, then he is truly a spiritual worker experientially.

Such a shift experientially and in consciousness should be cultivated daily. For without this cultivating one is studying the menu rather than eating the meal. If you freely choose to be in communion with the spiritual worlds, cultivating this practice is more important than any of the teachings. This is why an incarnate life—embodied existence—in order to facilitate such a shift, understand the importance of creating the right external circumstances as much as possible. For this work that we are doing together has more import or value than you can conceptually know.

There is a vast change happening in your galaxy. You don't know who you really are. Even your identity as a galactic being is not who you really are. Nonetheless you have intimate relationship with your own galaxy. Galaxies, too, form clusters. So through me there is a trans-galactic or multi-galactic energy. When one passes through the gate of death, one is closer to those dimensions that were further away when embodied. So in order for you to be closer to these trans-galactic dimensions, you need to be in communion with us. My final word: Understand even the best of your scientists, your cosmologists, understand very little. But some are moving in the right direction.

Blessings

Elucia

An Opening Conversation

"The flow of energy from fifth dimensional consciousness through fourth dimensional intellect and into third dimensional biological and physical experience is not only possible, but vital if humanity is to evolve on a habitable planet".

Bindo

... even though I am presently discarnate my love for this garden planet is full and unwavering. It is this fifth dimension that now beckons forth more potently than ever ...

I wish to clarify some important aspects of the ongoing descriptions regarding third, fourth and fifth dimensional embodiments or incarnations. Elucia described the third dimension as biological, fourth as human and fifth as spiritualised human, but what must be understood is that each greater dimension from an evolutionary perspective subsumes the lesser dimensions, and what this means is that the third and fourth dimensions are active within the fifth.

It can be described in such a way that we can talk of three major types of human incarnations, namely third, fourth or fifth-guided or dominated, and this is especially important to understand at this phase of radical transformation. Generally, most humans shift between these dimensions and yet it is so that there are dominating dimensions to the degree that we can loosely classify these three types. Those human incarnations that are guided by third dimensional impulses, in effect allow thinking and action to be led by biological drives and are essentially lesser evolved than non-human species. This is because although they have fourth dimensional human capacities, these are generally employed in the service of biological drives. This means that human thinking with its capacity to deviate in relative freedom from natural instinct, can combine biological drives, that humans share with all other species, with degrees of free thinking. This is the underlying explanation of fourth-dimensional humans led by third-dimensional drives.

The second type of human embodiment can be described as fourth dimensional-dominated and this implies a good degree of discipline and control over biological drives, but as such, unhealed and untransformed in contrast to fifth dimensional spiritualised potential. It is this fourth-dimensional evolutional stage, between biological drives and spirituality, that most humanity has been struggling within for some thousands of earth years.

The fifth dimensional-guided and motivated human incarnations have been as wondrous lights shining in the twilight. They have always been a guiding force on our beloved planet, including my own soul presence, and even though I am presently discarnate my love for this garden planet is full and unwavering. It is this fifth dimension that now beckons forth more potently than ever as increasing numbers of souls awaken to their true natures and missions. My contribution to these inter-dimensional transmissions is to delve deeply into the complex variations of these mixed dimensions and bring forth greater clarity that can help in the transitions underway within present humanity.

When souls in incarnated human embodiment allow third dimensional biological drives to dominate, they are, at best, akin to non-human species. Such human incarnations may be harmless, but they are essentially not contributing to human evolution. Others though, who are third dimensionally-dominated, are anything but harmless. The variety of third and fourth dimensional blends is limitless, and the same applies to fifth dimensional hybrids, because every human incarnation is actually a dimensional hybrid. Every human incarnation includes the fifth dimension, but if essentially latent and unconscious it is as if non-existent. A metaphor could be that of an artist that has produced nothing and doesn't even recognise the inner artistic capacity. It is like the fairy-tale of Sleeping Beauty awaiting the kiss of life.

It would be rare for a human being to be entirely dominated by third dimensionality, but it does happen. Some damaged bodies are in this state especially when brain damage is severe. In the context I am exploring with you it is fully biologically functioning humans under consideration, and it here that we need to comprehend how it is that a potential flower remains a stunted seed, and how to deal with this. The outer manifestations of this stuntedness are what you experience as the worst aspects of human behaviour. In eastern religions many of these demonic human tendencies are symbolically depicted in sculpture, canvas or scripture. They are the blood thirsty demons who lust after flesh and swing bloody swords by their sides, wearing necklaces of shrunken decapitated human heads. They represent an aspect of fourth dimensional mental depravity driven by third dimension biological drives that mutates a human incarnation into a servant of evil. Humans who are at the darkest end of the spectrum of evil, are those that block and disrupt evolutionary progress and cannot be destroyed by decapitation, because souls cannot be extinguished by eliminating their bodies, but rather they too must be brought back from the brink and gradually or dramatically spontaneously transfigured.

What needs to be contemplated is how energies at the high end of the spectrum, the fifth dimension influencing the fourth, flow through the fourth dimension influencing the third. This needs careful consideration. The best way to imagine flows through the spectrum is to think of how stronger energies influence all weaker energies. It is a more powerful flow than the reverse process, because stronger forces are more powerful than weaker forces. Contemplate the implications of this.

The key factor in this ever-changing spectrum of flows is consciousness, or to be precise, the degree to which consciousness is awakened and taking responsibility for its movements. Becoming aware of the changing flow of energies and consciousness requires a capacity to transcend surface energies and enter spaciousness and quietude. The deeper consciousness becomes, the less turbulence there is, and shifts the energy flows. This is an aspect of the science of consciousness that must be experientially explored beyond all theoretical speculation. Linguistic descriptions need to emerge from insight aided and inspired by actual experience and awareness of changing energy flows and their significance. It also needs to become a daily meditative and yogic process if there are to be profound practical effects. The flow of energy from fifth dimensional consciousness through fourth dimensional intellect and into third dimensional biological and physical experience is not only possible, but vital if humanity is to evolve on a habitable planet. There are two main ways to go about implementing the process described as flow from fifth to third dimension. The first way is dependent on your knowledge of how to achieve this one way or another, and therefore simply do so. This may involve motivation and choice, but knowledge is intact. The second way requires the honest acknowledgement that one doesn't have the necessary knowledge and therefore must seek for a guide or teacher who can initiate one into such gnosis. Is it that simple? Yes and no. It could be, but human tendencies can move towards inconsistent swings in flow, and moreover complex multi-dimensional variations, suggest that either of the two main ways outlined are easier said than done.

Elucia emphasised the importance of the will as a determining factor in the evolution of consciousness and its expression in embodied action. The question of importance therefore is, 'How do I strengthen my will?' You do not strengthen the will forces by force. Will forces are transpersonal. You come to the Father by way of the Son, but the Son must consciously sacrifice his own imaginary autonomy. If you do not know how to sacrifice your mind to Supreme empty Consciousness, then honestly seek for someone who can initiate you. If you do know how to sacrifice your mind to Supreme empty Consciousness, activate the will and pass through the portal.

Krishnaji

Freedom is a prime inherent principle that is the very essence of Consciousness itself.

My contribution must always be finely directed towards one prime aim: that of the absolute and uncompromising freedom of thought, but this should never be misunderstood as license to think anything you want, and immediately it would seem we face a paradox here, or worse, an absurdity.

Absolute freedom of thought only applies to the natural mind when it is free of all obscuration and defilement. This pure state can also be described as innocent and sacred consciousness. It is this pure mind that is capable of great thought and worthy of the best humanity can produce. Not every person can clear layers of programmed and conditioned thought and thereby think with a free mind. My efforts over vast historical time have been concentrated on freeing the mind of all unfree thought. That is my mission.

What does it mean to think freely for oneself? Follow this carefully. Look within your own mind. What of your thoughts are freely your own, meaning without cultural, religious, nationalistic, or other social and historical indoctrination? My intention in contributing in this way is simply to awaken souls to their inherent potential of pure mind and independent thought.

AN OPENING CONVERSATION

In the eighth century Adi Shankaracharya travelled across the breadth and width of the Indian sub-continent debating with scholars and others. His aim, like mine was to free the mind from false understanding. In this mission, unlike most others, no particular methods or rituals were suggested.

Freedom does not belong to a separate entity alone, whether human or god. A sense of separated freedom is limited and only a shadow of true freedom. True freedom is in alignment with universal nature and is purposeful, but only to the degree as it evolves as expressions of universal intelligence. In other words, freedom in its truest value behaves as a conduit of cosmos. This perspective accepts that cosmos has an inherent intelligence and purpose. Other perspectives can deny that we exist in an intelligent and purposeful cosmos, where understanding freedom would be perceived as radically different to that which I am positing. Freedom at its purest belongs to cosmos of which personhood is a fractal microcosm. Another way to approach this is to imagine freedom as the calm, still depths of the ocean and limited freedom as the surface which is subject to all manner of changing circumstances. It is all one ocean but the experience of varying depths differs.

The universe is holographic and projective. When understanding and describing deeper experiences, it can be confusing to use language appropriate to the surface. My use of language generally bypasses words such as dimensionality and other words that tend to separate. My perception and experience is holistic so I avoid words that suggest division and separateness. Freedom is a prime inherent principle that is the very essence of Consciousness itself. This principle matures into a self-reflective mind that can move into Source and out from Source into free thinking. It is Source thinking through an outsourced holographic manifestation of itself, from timelessness into time, and spaciousness into space. Mind can be intermediary between depths of one seamless Supreme Being. The author is engaging with me and a host of others in this dialectic. This is because the topic of freedom touches on the profoundest mystery of cosmos. This in itself will help to shape this manuscript. My incarnational tendency has been such that engagements with others have sharpened my inner experience and intellectual capacity to a tremendous degree. This developed into a unique personality configuration. The author is allowing contrasting perspectives to play into my own. Another soul intimately involved in this ongoing investigation is David, who will contribute shortly.

Pure mind has embodied and mind has therefore followed into an illusion of separateness that only exists as a reality within physical life. But as this is a part of the evolution emanating from Source it has a divine purpose. The harmonising of infinite and finite is the purpose. The recognition of infinity by mind that is an outgrowth of infinity is a part of the purpose. The translation, so to speak, of Infinity's language into embodied existence is a part of the purpose. And the freedom of mind to experientially discover sacred freedom truly aligned with Source is a part of the purpose.

Choosing freely how to share this sacred knowledge is an expression of embodied human purpose, mirroring a prime motivation of Source. This must be maturely psychologically self-realized. Mercurius was half-human, half-God. Being such he was known as the winged one, as he had small wings on his feet which allowed him to travel freely between the realms of Gods and humans. He was therefore able to act as intermediary. He was of course known to the Romans as Mercury, the God of communication. This is where human consciousness resides. Humans cannot reach to where the Gods reside, nor can Gods reach to where humans dwell, but there is a middle zone where both can go, and there they can communicate with each other.

David

If consciousness realizes its unity as a singular phenomenon, freedom cannot be anything other than cosmically aligned.

I am delighted to be a contributor. My incarnational biography is one of attempting to cross-fertilize spirituality and science. This included a fascination with understanding consciousness and quantum theory. In regards to the topic of freedom I do not know if I have anything remarkable to add, but I shall try to add something useful.

Linking freedom to cosmic intelligence is paradoxical from one point of view. If freedom needs to be aligned with cosmic intelligence then how free is it? This apparent paradox or even contradiction in terms can only be clearly understood if we acknowledge our interdependence and inherent interbeingness. Autonomous freedom would then be perceived as an illusion, or at least an inferior and limited type of freedom. This is counter-intuitive to consciousness that believes it is a separate entity. But if consciousness realizes its unity as a singular phenomenon, freedom cannot be anything other than cosmically aligned. What type of freedom would it be if your planet decided to go it alone and remove itself from your solar system? Or your legs decided to walk off in opposite directions? Freedom then belongs to a greater order that, like bees, functions in accord with a vaster destiny and reality.

Quantum reality also adds a vital perspective to the topic of freedom. Freedom is not only aligned within your space-time linear reality but also with inter-dimensional simultaneity. This can be approached as Carl Jung suggested by understanding synchronicity or by advances in quantum science. Where we discarnate souls are, this is the prime reality. Freedom here is immediate and intentional. By way of immediate intentionality it is choiceless. Incarnated souls can experience freedom in both linear and lateral modes. Indeed human consciousness is the fulcrum where all energies can meet. The wondrous allurement of incarnated freedom embraces all possibilities, potentially. It is the purpose within the evolution of consciousness.

Krishnaji 2

When consciousness moves in the direction of accepting that choices are significant, a very different reality begins to take shape.

It is Krishnaji here again.

Humans can freely choose just about anything they want to. The question I freely want to pose is this: Is there any significance to the choices made? If there is, why is that so? If there isn't any significance then it really doesn't matter what choices are made.

This question aims at the hub of your humanitarian crisis. One view is that choices have no real significance in the big picture. Choices have consequences and that is that. We are all responsible for our choices and their consequences. Significance in this view is a personal matter and simply a way of choosing moment by moment without greater considerations. This is close to the way it is for most humans. If I choose a particular restaurant to eat in and then choose a meal from the menu, then the significance is my experience alone. There are many who view all of life in that way. The question, 'Are choices significant?' can only be answered by the individual, but one fact is self-evident: every choice has consequences. Therefore, are consequences significant? Within every moment, consciousness experiences both consequences and choices. Any authentic understanding of karma includes choice and consequence. The choice to perceive anything in a particular way is a choice too and also has consequences. If this fact is insignificant then nothing matters. If nothing matters life itself is rendered insignificant. To reach such a position is a choice too, but not one that I choose. And yet an insight emerges with this consideration. The part of consciousness that would be tempted to adopt such an existentially absurd position is the part that wants to choose freely anything it wants without consideration of any consequences. It is this potential within consciousness that is shocking to consider but must be acknowledged if it is to be overcome and transformed.

When consciousness moves in the direction of accepting that choices are significant, a very different reality begins to take shape. The question looms again, 'Why are choices significant?' One part of the response can be: 'Because choices have consequences and consequences are significant.' Consequences are what constitute the actual facts of life: either as an incarnated or discarnated being a choice is made. Life is significant. Think of the Creator asking, 'Is creating a universe significant?' If it isn't, then why choose to do it? The universe is you and you are the universe. Therefore this question is yours. How you answer in freedom is your choice and so will be the consequences.

Keith

Ground Zero consciousness takes on any form, any idea, any temporary role, and defines itself accordingly. In this way consciousness loses itself in its own creation.

'Ground Zero' is a grand metaphor for what happens inwardly when all the lies are stripped away, and at this moment a choice can be made with tremendous implications for the future. The choice is whether to continue to lie or begin telling the truth. Much of our civilisation is either based on lies or at least compromised by them. Lies have become the societal norm. What is meant by 'lies' is nuanced and complex, with various forms of intentional and unintentional deceptions, illusions, ulterior motives, half-truths and superficiality, often simply parading as something it is not.

This is true both at a personal level and collectively. When enough people engage in a similar way of thinking and doing, it becomes inculturated. Ground Zero, psychologically, is when all the obscurations to the innermost truth are removed. The reason why this is so important now is because history has caught up with us, globally. Gaia is under serious threat. James

Lovelock warned us about this threat, and now we are collectively in the midst of its unfolding. The cabal (those who most know what is happening, at least symptomatically, and have the power to respond) have engaged in a process of reactivity that has been mostly hidden from the masses. And this in itself is a great flaw. Because Ground Zero demands a trust in transparency, honesty and inclusivity. We are experiencing everywhere in today's world a complex network of non-transparency, dishonesty and segregation.

A principle is at play here. That which causes a problem cannot resolve it; it requires a change at Ground Zero, at the deepest level of consciousness. The hope is that enough people are awakening to the 'Great lies' and that the lies themselves are so incoherent that they assists in such an awakening. Ground Zero is about facing reality and truth telling. It is also an impulse that overthrows all that is obstructing the truth. This is both profoundly personal and collective. Truth and courage must with kindness and compassion, overturn the old order and initiate an authentic new age. And when this choice translates into external action, a new world is possible, founded on truth.In Goethe's Faust, Doctor Faust makes a deal with Mephistopheles (the Devil) and then plays out the consequences. This is another grand metaphor for our personal and collective situations. Deal-making is how Mephistopheles traps us. It is how we betray ourselves. We do a deal thinking that the promise of having our desires fulfilled will bring us happiness. This can be a collective desire, as in a vision of a better world. But a truly better world would involves inner transformation. It would not merely be a desire to survive. It would have a moral heart. It is an authentic and natural moral consciousness that alone can transform us as human individuals and humanity as a whole. I know this as an inner truth. I also know the struggle with Mephistopheles. We all do.

Ground Zero is one metaphor among many that points to a fundamental self-evident reality. Within the complex multidimensional human totality, there is an observing consciousness that is both personal and transpersonal. In its purest state it is empty of content. It is often referred to as 'I Am', because I can cognise I, as a conscious, aware Being. It is this Aware Being that we all have in common. Everything we think, feel and do emerges from this Consciousness: literally from empty infinity into finite forms, except that we are usually unaware of this fact. Ground Zero consciousness takes on any form, any idea, any temporary role, and defines itself accordingly. In this way consciousness loses itself in its own creation. Doctor Faust made a pact with the Lord of Illusions. He exchanged his autonomy for an imaginary belief that satisfying his desires would bring him happiness. Only Freedom in a homeostasis with discipline and commitment can restore the soul of Faust and awaken him out of his great dream. It is out of Ground Zero that Creator's intentions and impulses have arisen as cosmic and terrestrial nature, and then as conscious, aware beings that can emulate the Creator by way of free will. Freedom to think and choose is at the epicenter of the human condition.

Every human created manifestation has its cause in thinking. The entirety of human evolution is a process of human thinking and its consequences. Ground Zero is a metaphor indicating the primary responsibility of thinking as the active power within consciousness; an omnipotent and omni-present power that determines all external human created phenomena. Individually and collectively, thinking shapes the world we exist in. In the Old Testament of the Bible, it is written that 'humans' have 'dominion' over all of nature. 'Dominion' in this context has two possible interpretations. Firstly, that humans (mankind) are superior to unthinking nature and can therefore do what they want. Or secondly, because humans are thinking beings, they can act as stewards or caretakers of nature. Only in the latter sense can we perceive a moral imperative. Here we can become aware of the threshold between moral and immoral thinking and the choice to align and cultivate either. The local and global situation humanity finds itself in is a result of an ongoing process of thinking. But thinking is free to choose what it thinks. Consciousness in its active mode, is influenced by inner and outer forces, and yet can take hold of its true status as autonomous Ground Zero, as 'I Am', as conscious sovereign reality, the moral centre of Being. Thinking can enlighten itself through immediate revelatory insights into the nature of consciousness itself. And thinking can become a truly compassionate, loving and wise steward. Such a mind can transform itself and the world. It can play cricket instead of war.

Parelsitis

... this approach to healing the traumas of humanity [Metaphorical Psychology] will be inaugurated into the new paradigm of consciousness as your twenty-first century unfurls.

Much of what you think and express is metaphorical in nature without it being realized as such. Metaphors, like myths, are pictorial or symbolic ways of expressing underlying realities, truths, principles or archetypes that ordinary rational language finds difficult or impossible to convey.

When this belongs to 'vertical dissonance' or unintegrated inter-dimensional experience, metaphors become disorganized and seemingly inappropriate. This can become so inwardly chaotic that your modern scientific materialistic and largely atheistic perspective can deem it psychotic, manic, depressive or bi-polar. Metaphorical psychology can approach this vertical dissonance from an inter-dimensional perspective. Inter-dimensional experiences are at the best of times difficult to apprehend and comprehend for human embodied souls. This topic belongs to the evolutional transition your human species is passing through.

Metaphors are attempts to understand and express what the rational ego-mind cannot, that is until a mature degree of integrated understanding has occurred. It is this approach to healing the traumas of humanity that will be inaugurated into the new paradigm of consciousness as your twenty-first century unfurls.

The beginnings of a new psychology are underway. Many souls have helped to prepare the way, not only in the field of psychology, but other related disciplines. Indeed a great confluence of rivers is emerging, far ahead of your corporate institutions, politics, media, education, health and almost every part of the ordinary daily existence of the vast majority of your population. This can shroud in populist propaganda what is happening among the growing leading edge pioneers of your potential collective destiny.

When anything or anyone is in an unsustainable process, eventually a breakdown heralds a breakthrough. When metaphorical psychology gains a sound foothold within your Western culture, you can be sure a breakthrough is happening, a changing of the guard.

Merged Voices

A Soul Cluster Collaboration

"Those who repeatedly incarnate as reality or light-harbingers continue to experiment with ways of communication and expression, and this is an ongoing evolutional transcarnational process"

Life, Death and Freedom

All contributors will now merge their voices.

Freud named the death wish 'Thanatos' after the Greek God of mortal death. This daemon represents a part of consciousness and Freud was correct in pointing out its place in the pantheon of powers embedded in human consciousness and subconsciousness. In Eastern religions Gods and Goddesses representing death are substantially represented, but to Freud Thanatos was more than simply death symbolism, it was a 'death wish.' It was an element that chose to destroy life. When this element remains within the unconscious it can lure unsuspecting victims to untimely and often tragic deaths. But how could it be that a death wish that includes the universe is greater than the desire for life? In Hinduism the word 'Lila' means something like God's play. Krishna delighted in the created natural world. This is our eternal playground: Shambhala, the mythic Promised Land. It is the potential of human evolution. This is why the creative living impulse is stronger than Thanatos. Yet the principle of freedom requires that consciousness must freely choose. Consciousness must overcome its own darker tendencies, not by avoidance but by freely choosing love over hate, life over death.

The hundredth-monkey metaphor goes something like this: it is only when the hundredth monkey says or does something that an observable event takes place. The ninety-nine monkey steps were hardly noticed, but all led to monkey step one-hundred, and 'boom!', the event happens. Every monkey has played its part, but the hundredth monkey tends to get the credit. This metaphor applies to life and death outcomes, for example an outcome that is experienced as wonderful or one that is considered terrible. In other words outcomes are consequences that have reached a certain observable manifestation, like ripe fruit ready to be picked. Events such as suicide do not happen out of nothing. Humanity, individually or collectively exists in an ever-flowing present where consciousness feeds into either constructive or destructive processes with choices made.

The question, 'How free are your choices?' requires a complex response. When many monkeys all jump in a similar way a pattern emerges which can become quite addictive. The hundredth monkey is like a culminating point, a karmic outcome, not an end itself but an observable manifestation, The manifestation has many choices and consequences hidden in its mostly untold biography. But "monkeys" do not need to follow each other in addictive-forming ways. Neural pathways can deviate. Consciousness can jump ship and swim ashore. Recognising consciousness as a creative power, an awakening can occur whereby consciousness can reprogram itself. Freedom is as freedom does. A self- evident fact that is revolutionary for an incarnated soul who has lost the motivation to live. Life is Creator's Lila! A torus is an energy vortex that continuously swirls and changes as elements are attracted to or fly away from it. Discarnate souls can merge into a singular torus energy field. Incarnate souls can do this too but because of individuated bodies and personalities the challenge is far more difficult. Imagine a cyclone with a calm centre whirling across space attracting and pulling into itself many elements that cannot resist its force. Now imagine two cyclones: one that is oriented towards love and harmony, the other towards hatred and war. Choices made are as steps towards either cyclone. Humanity struggles between two cyclonic forces. Choices are significant if you care about what cyclone you want to identify with and incrementally become a part of. The hundredth monkey is the symbolic cyclone entry point Every monkey step is significant.

Complexity and Contextuality

Complexity reaches its zenith within human incarnation. Evolution increases complexity and becomes mirrored both internally and externally. There are simple elements that can be interwoven to make living with complexity easier. This is a difficult topic to communicate about but a necessary one. Complexity is multi-dimensional and, rather like a kaleidoscope, constantly changing in unpredictable ways. Modern incarnated life for most of humanity is complex. Patterns emerge and change from moment to moment, day to day. What seems certain becomes uncertain. What isn't even on the radar suddenly appears. It can all seem random and often chaotic. Even when a sense of order occurs there can still be uncertainty. Multiple aspects combine and re-combine and every new move, rather like in a chess game, alters the game. This is the reality within fourth dimensional linear existence.

But there are higher dimensions, within which exists a higher natural organising process. Guiding forces flowing through and into the lower dimensions. Fourth dimensional consciousness cannot control those forces. The habit-forming and analytical mind often messes with natural ordering. There is wisdom that would allow the river of life to flow at the right pace and in such a way that it reaches the ocean. When this happens complexity no longer seems chaotic. The natural flow may not go where you expect. It is unpredictable but if surrendered to in trust would take you where you are meant to go. Opportunities that are linked to life's flow and are receptive to guiding forces are like portals that open and invite you to pass through. Suddenly everything becomes in service to spirit. Miraculously higher spiritual frequencies weave through fourth dimensional complexity and a path unfolds. One must simply not push or pull the river. It has its own natural pace. Do what is there to do at this moment. Complexity and contextuality co-exist. There are no fixed rules or truths in fourth-dimensional complexity because contexts continually change. Any singular element introduced into a complex situation will alter the context. Context within fourth dimensionality is a key phenomenon to contemplate and allow insights to emerge from.

We will offer a few examples.

Any organisation is complex. Imagine one organisation of whatever size. It consists of various individuals who have designated roles. For the organisation to hold together it needs to be organised. Behind the organising principle there are goals, visions and projected outcomes. There are also motivations. There are agreed upon rules and operational guidelines. There are individual temperaments, skill-levels and personalities. There are relationship dynamics. All this and more belongs to complexity. Contextuality refers to the ever-changing complexity. What is important to grasp about contextuality is that complexity cannot be viewed or understood rigidly. There can be no deeper understanding about complex systems without regard to changing context. So what does context inform us about? A smaller example can be a family. Parents agree to an outing that the children are really looking forward to. Then an unexpected situation arises that prevents the outing from happening. The children are of course disappointed. They may be angry and blame the parents for the cancelled outing. One child may have cancelled a concert because of this expected family outing. All this can be complex, but the context changed. This is fourth dimensional life. Space-time incarnated existence is unpredictable and ever-changing. Change happens inwardly too, within the individual. For example, someone agrees to go somewhere at a certain time, but then doesn't feel to when the time arrives. A change of inner experience or perspective has changed the context. But this could degenerate into unreliability, so fifth-dimensional space is required too. It is just like navigating a wild river. You do not know what is ahead. The river environment keeps changing.

The way to navigate through complexity and contextuality is to be fluid and flexible. For the individual, a meditatively qualitative practice is invaluable. Without inner space any potential fifth dimensional insights are either blocked or distorted. Think of a radio station not properly attuned. Inner transformational work is essentially concerned with 'clearing' incarnational static. Bring this evolving clarity into fourth-dimensional activity and you have possible models for organisations having real integrity and compassionate, sane outcomes.

Conspiracy, Lies and Deception

These transmissions have reached to where questions should be invited from the author or any other incarnated participants. In this way we can open to inter-dimensional dialogues as practice runs for common future human evolvement.

Leanne has been watching a filmed interview from filmmaker Stanley Kubrick recorded three days before his death and withheld by his own wish for fifteen years after his passing. In this interview he confesses that he had made the film of America's moon landing and therefore it had never happened. This has prompted Leanne to ask about conspiracies and lies.

Conspiracies have one essential element in common: they are all motivated by self-interest. When two or more conscious entities form an alliance based on narrow self-interest, places its own agenda ahead of the greater good, and 'conspires' to deceive and lie to achieve its aims, a conspiracy is hatched. Of course, some entities can be motivated by positive desires, but are nonetheless conspirational if they lie and deceive, or in other words, are involved in collective attempts at deceptive hidden agendas or motives. A conspiracy appears when two or more entities consciously agree to partake in secretive actions, and this then manifests as an external phantasm.

Conspiracies are always elitist in that they conspire against others, motivated by an in-group psychology and intentionality.

Conspiracies breed lies in their wake. The first principle of a successful conspiracy is that the agreements remain hidden from public view. Only the in-group know the truth and even then if it is complex many only know as much as is deemed necessary. Conspiracies can be as small as two people conspiring together or as large as international conspiracies that have agendas as large and as complex as anything you can imagine. Then there are inter-dimensional conspiracies that we shall not delve into here.Once a conspiracy has been established it is not so easy to undo. Why not? Let us ask a question first. Does a conspiracy lead to deception or do deceptions lead to conspiracies? The fact is that a conspiracy is an agreement by two or more entities to deceive others. Once this agreement has been enacted, consequences follow. A lie becomes more complex as it evolves.

When a conspiracy involves large numbers of people and organisations, the web of lies creates a layered phantasm almost impossible to see through. This may be so, but there is one weakness that every conspiracy has and cannot overcome. This is the Achilles heel of all conspiracies. 'The truth will set you free'. Disclosure can be discredited and thwarted by many means but its omnipresent potential is the conspirator's worst fear: and its capacity to 'blow the lid off the lie' the conspirator's worst nightmare.

There are two ways that manifestations of conspiracies can be transformed into clear, transparent and ethical representations of fifth dimensionally inspired outcomes. One way is to gradually work within corrupted structures. These structures are not necessarily evil but they lack transparency and inclusiveness. They are founded upon secret dealings and elitist self-interests. The consequences of conspiracies are extremely varied as are the motives driving them, but even at best, they lack the universalism and truthfulness that is the potential inherent within future humanity. Transparency, when guided by fifth dimensional wisdom and humility, allows for truthful expression and communication. There are no ulterior motives and what you see is what there is. All movements towards such an ideal are sanctioned by Spirit. Therefore gradualism is the way to carefully and wisely work within structures and this is one way to bring about change.

The other way is for entire structures to collapse. Such an outcome may be consciously chosen but more often it happens as a result of unsustainable and unstable inner forces, a bit like a building collapsing because the internal structures have been weakened irreparably. This allows for a clean slate, so to speak, but if the same entities are recreating new structures, conspirational and dishonest elitism will build new towers destined for the same fate as the one that has collapsed.

Consider what transparency implies. If children were guided to understand transparency they would be less vulnerable to social conditioning that gradually moulds them into agents of future conspiracies, lies and deceptions. For that to happen, social structures need to be transformed. And in order for that to happen, individuals must choose to transform.

The good news is that increasing numbers of individuals, groups and organizations are moving in the right direction. And paradoxically, the universe conspires to bring light into the darkness!

Transparent Collaboration

What happens when entities conspire? A field of impressions is created, deceptive impressions that distort the external representation, much like a magic show. The very word 'conspire' conjures a secretive collaboration aiming to deceive, even if by omission. Transparent collaboration, in contrast, sets up a field of impressions approximating truth. Things are more or less what they seem to be.

Historically, the justification to either conspire collaboratively or collaborate transparently has been complex, contextual, and without strict moral boundaries. For example, within many ancient mystery schools, conspiracies were aimed at protecting practices and wisdom from the unprepared. Transparency would have had most unwise consequences.

This is still true to some degree, but in your technological age, the act of conspiring to deceive has become so widespread and embedded into all aspects of your global culture, it threatens to destroy your human civilisation and planetary biosphere. The manipulation of media especially uses vast networks of conspirational collaborations, such as corporate and celebrity influence to cast a field of illusions, lies and deceptions. Just like a magic spell. this field is a phantasmagoria that never is what it seems to be. The conspirational environment has created a virtual second reality that has infiltrated every corner of your fourth dimensional field. Transparent collaboration is a force fundamentally at variance with this ingrained nest of illusions, deceptions and lies. The hidden vested interests and ulterior motives driving conspiracies are opposed simply by the presence of transparent collaboration. Let it be understood that any evolutional movement towards fifth dimensional guided and manifested human civilisation must embrace models of universal transparent collaboration. Historical contextual justifications for collaborative conspiracies do not belong to the future evolution of humanity, if it is to survive. Souls will evolve according to this division of essential archetypes. The two types will no longer be able to share a common environment.

In the meantime, there will be transitional processes where hybrids of these two orientations will exist within complex contextual circumstances. The dominance of collaborative conspiracies is such that it cannot be vanquished easily. Knowing your own individual orientation and working to implement transparent collaboration as much as is wisely possible is most important. This is certainly a part of the great work now happening in your world.

Inner Collaborative Transparency

Everything external mirrors inner patterns. Therefore collaborative conspiracies and transparent collaborations occur within individuated consciousness. Related to this is the fact that the human psyche is divided into multiple streams. As with all externalities change must also happen inwardly. An inner collaborative conspiracy can be simple or complex, conscious or sub-conscious, but always follows the essential principle of parts of self conspiring to bring about a particular outcome, against the wishes of other parts. Without delving into the sheer complexity of this syndrome of the 'divided self', more importantly, let us look at the inner movement into transparent collaboration.

When the individuated psyche begins to be radically honest a healing of inner divisions takes place. One is literally connecting parts of one's inner organisation clearly and coherently. This process of inner integration creates a foundation upon which external changes can be inspired. This inner-outer model is what represents health: health for an individual psyche and for external manifestations. It is as simple as this, in theory. Both inner and outer collaborative processes operate through time-space and incrementally build into various outcomes. This is an omnipresent reality governed by consciousness. The state of consciousness is the creator for all that occurs mentally and manifestly. Consciousness, with its karmic legacy implanted within multi-dimensional layers of individuated self, does not transform in one huge event. The same applies to external structures. And yet, as consciousness is the agent of change, change occurs omnipresently. Self-awareness is the key.

Incremental processes can remind us of the 'hundred monkey' metaphor. The question therefore can be asked, 'What hundredth monkey are we progressing towards?' The following quote is from a book Keith is writing. We would like to respond and integrate this into our collaboration.

"Something must happen in the best way, but we cannot create this by ego, yet we cannot avoid it either. This must happen. We can choose to avoid egos over dominating tendencies as much as possible. Ego didn't create the galaxies and nature. There is a natural unfolding of spirit. We can be very powerful according to how we surrender to Supreme power. If ego takes hold of this power it becomes immediately restricted. This is a part of spiritual practice!"

The human ego is like the surface of a lake. It constantly changes depending on the weather and other factors. It believes it is the entire lake. This is the problem. It is only the surface and as such has very limited powers. Ego is an outcome of nature just as everything else is. Surrendering to greater powers is the way for ego to become powerful itself, and what is referred to as 'Supreme power' implies surrendering to Source. This cannot be done easily in a pure way but we can choose to avoid ego's dominating tendencies as a spiritual practice. The words, 'This is a part of spiritual practice' are potent. This is the way to invite fifth dimensional transformations into fourth dimensional mind and action. It is the essential hub of spiritual practice because it is the act of transcendence rather than the concept or theory. Ego in its restrictive tendencies is sometimes a type of forgetfulness. The greatest restrictive tendency is possibly when ego takes credit for its own power. Spiritual unfoldment works quite well in the cosmos: the galaxies continue to evolve and expand without self-destructing. Earthly nature follows in its bountiful manner. Only human ego in its disconnected separation and bloated hubris strays from Spirit's way.

The Battle between Two Forces

There is a battle. This fact must be acknowledged. The battle is internal and therefore external. It is essentially a battle between two forces. These two forces do not belong together. They are antithetical. The syndrome of 'us and them' is both authentic and false. Authentically the 'us and them' belongs to an inner dichotomy that projects externally. Fifth-dimensional consciousness and embodiment would be, 'All things bright and beautiful, for Lord God made them all.' Homo-spiritus would have transformed all darkness into light. As long as incarnated souls are untransformed an inner battle yet reigns, of which the outer battles are manifestations. Being aware of untransformed inner dichotomy is an authentic acknowledgement of the battle. Then external manifestations can be understood in their true context. The battle is especially fought in your present era in the field of information. You dwell amidst myriads of information bytes and bites and, more than ever before, discernment is needed. Misinformation and disinformation are rife. It is a fact that cultivating a capacity to engage in 'active research' is most important. The battle is fought in all parts of your global society, consciously and unconsciously.

Even in ancient times this battle was understood as the essential evolutional challenge for humanity. It has its origins in the hybrid breeding programs that are now hidden behind myth and folklore. When different strands of genetic material are mixed, as in inter-species interbreeding or in this context different humanoid sub-species, one aspect of the new constitution can be far more advanced than another. This is both a boon and a risk to evolutional development. You are facing this too with your genetically modified crops. But the legacy of genetic mixing and cloning is not new. Humanity itself is an outcome of various interbreeding programs. It is this that is responsible for the battle of forces experienced both historically and at your present time. The risk can now be understood with degrees of sophistication and accessibility impossible in the historical past. The same is true for the tremendous creative possibilities now on offer to humanity. Risks are meaningful only in context and even then are complicated. The risks involved in evolutional engineering are essentially those related to unnatural hybrids. In other words, a creative universe where entities can consciously intervene especially in order to propel evolution in chosen directions, but with unpredictable consequences. This is the type of universe we belong to.

Supreme Source is a risk taker. The essential risk was always going to be that entities could choose unwisely. In freedom an entity chose individuated power. This created a relationship of the first type: that of between Source and other. This was allowed, and Source became known as the great mother. The power of the other, also known as the Prodigal son, allowed the first type of choice and the first type of risk. First types are also known as archetypes. They always retain their original quality.

This first choice was between aligning with, or deviating from Source. The first deviation is also known as original sin, which also means 'missing the mark.' All further deviations stem from this decision to separate from Source in a non-aligned way. Choosing to remain aligned with Source is the original meaning of 'ethical' and 'moral'. In this universal context it means doing the right thing according to an alignment to Source. Individuated power granted by Source therefore instigated a tremendous prime 'signature' quality of our universe and of human consciousness. The inherent risk was the entire potential spectrum of consequences deriving from choosing to deviate from Source's nature and intentionality. This natural intentionality is what Australian Aborigines refer to as the 'Dreamtime.' The nature of this is also known as 'Kanyini.' In Western early Christian and pre-Christian times it was sometimes known as Gnosis.

All these archetypes play on, like original cosmic tunes within the complexity of modern human societies. Omnipotence is the original granting of freedom for individuated power Omniprescence is the constant potential to choose alignment to or divergence from Source. Omniscience is the capacity to know the choice and to consciously choose. The risk is an archetype too. Both choices lead to consequences, or karma. This is the anatomy of your inner constitution now as it has always been ever since the divine granting of freedom.

Imitation

One main form of deviation from Source is imitation. There are two types of imitation, one benign and the other deviant. Benign imitation is how newly incarnated beings learn and grow by observing others. In its more sophisticated forms such imitation belongs to the topic of resonance, but more about this later. Deviant imitation is an altogether different topic. It is essentially a type of spiritual immaturity and/or separatist manipulation In other words, a self-deception or a lie. We need to look more deeply into both these types.

Self-deceptions of a spiritual type can be naivety or forms of denial. They are not conscious lies. Naivety is a way of not knowing any better. Denial is more consciously 'not wanting to know any better.' This becomes types of sub-conscious or repressed knowledge. Imitative behavior then is self-deceived and capable of deceiving others. By contrast, conscious manipulative tendencies engender lies. Conscious lying in service of imitative spirituality is a form of evil. In reality both types of imitation as here explained tend to be entangled but with definite leanings one way or the other. Spiritual maturity is then to be understood as consciousness without blemish.

In Buddhism blemishes are sometimes known as defilements. They are tendencies that essentially belong to naivety, self-deception or lying. They can also be known as lower human nature. These tendencies have evolved into sophisticated webs of subterfuge and manipulation, fuelled by separatist self-interest. Imitation really means consciously, sub-consciously or unconsciously presenting to be something one isn't. Only genuine inner practices and penetrating contemplative insights can weaken and transform these deviated tendencies.

Awakening to Reality

The evolved human brain is an awesome wonder of cosmic evolution. It has developed with the help of interstellar interventions to master sophisticated levels of communication and imagination. In other words, humans can think just about whatever they choose. This is in reality a God-like power. The human mind is in reality an emanation of Source. It is Source believing it is human. The risk was and is that mind can move in any direction within the realms of infinite possibilities. Human evolution is a testimony and legacy of human mental power. When this power is unleashed without wise guardianship the potential risk manifests as conglomerates of illusory phantasmagorias. We shall express this in another way because it is vital for spiritual aspirants to gain insights into this. The human mind easily and normally suffers from perceptual and conceptual myopia or tunnel vision. This conditioned and largely ingrained condition obscures reality and replaces it with networks of illusions that attempt to coherently justify an assumptive position. The intellectual capacity to link things in seemingly coherent ways allows for almost any belief to be upheld within its own context, but contextual complexity itself always implies that reality is beyond any such limited myopic boundaries.

We can give you an example based on real events but put together imaginatively to help make the point. There are two people who view the same something in very different ways. Their differences make them into perceived enemies. In their individual ways they go to great lengths to justify their opposing positions but as adversaries. Then a third person comes along who is a bridge builder. He doesn't want to take sides but moreover he sees strengths and weaknesses within both positions. The more he researches into both positions the more complexity he becomes aware of but also begins to have insights as to how a bridge could be built between them. The problem is that within the complexity there is much misinformation and disinformation. There are also emotional reactions and defensive aggressive tendencies. There is history. There is entangled karma. There may be social dimensions involved that outreach simple inter-relational dynamics. The bridge builder has a great challenge at hand. Where does one begin? This to one degree or another is where we all stand. We conform to one version of reality and perceive those who do not conform to our perspective, as enemies or irrelevant. What reality will transcend conflict and indifference?

There is an archetypal person. His/her name is Everyone. Everyone seeks for reality that is without blemish. We refer here to this as spiritual reality or fifth-dimensional reality. It is reality beyond division. Everyone discovers this. It is transformational and beyond comparison. The challenge now is to bring others to this experience and insight. Everyone tries to do this in particular ways because there is no other way to do this in the finite human realm. Incarnation after incarnation Everyone tries to bring others to a realization of reality, in various and particular ways. Some of these ways become world religions, others become stories, rituals, myths, parables, music, art and every possible way to mirror reality to a humanity caught in webs of divisive illusion and distorted, unclear perception. Everyone incarnates as everybody but only a few have awakened to reality, and of them only a few have tried to bring others to it. Those who repeatedly incarnate as reality or light-harbingers continue to experiment with ways of communication and expression, and this is an ongoing evolutional transcarnational process. The followers of such souls often then bring the teachings down into the divisive realm of human myopia.

What you need to be aware of is that gradually increasing numbers of souls are being brought closer to self-awakening and beyond the divisive and conflictual baggage of history. The historical tendency to form select groups with associated secret in-house knowledge and techniques must be superseded. Universalism must not become another elite group. Consciousness must realize the common denominator that binds all living beings. This must happen if human evolution on your planet is to continue. We are here to help.

The Challenge

It is not an easy challenge. You literally exist in two interwoven realms: that of being everyone and someone. It can also be expressed as no-one and someone. Universal and personal co-exist and must become as merged voices. Your challenge is made difficult because your global culture reflects somebody-type myopia. The evolved blessing of individuality has become a complex curse. Smaller interests have all but blotted out greater perspectives. You dwell within a global prison-house of mental myopia.

And yet it is akin to Jesus the Christ walking among the deluded and ignorant. We are all potentially Jesus and Gautama walking in the wilderness where few hear our true voices. This is how it may appear, but to a trained overview and evolutional sight another understanding can emerge. It is true that we dwell within the midst of history's complex consequences. It is true that we have inherited the dross of human ignorance and stupidity. But it is also true that an evolution of consciousness has been incrementally building. The voices of universal love, compassion, creativity and intelligence have largely been banished and unheard.

Now you enter the great transition. The voices of ignorance and stupidity are now critically endangered. Their collective empires have become so unstable and unsustainable that the entire structure is in imminent danger of catastrophic collapse. This is the crack in the wall that allows light to shine through. An example is that an idea that is lampooned and laughed at can suddenly be taken seriously, such as climate change. There is a rebellious response happening. Many souls feel as if they have been waiting for this 'time' for eons, a time when creative universal voices are heeded and rejoiced in. The challenge is not easy because the leadership of your global institutions is still mostly in the hands of old paradigm materialists, but there is a groundswell of consciousness-raising occurring. This cannot be stopped. The survival impulse will sway even those who are narcissistically engaged in narrow self-interest.

The situation is critical and must be fought inwardly if one is to impact externally. This is our trans-dimensional challenge: we who as a cluster love the creative unfoldment of life on your beautiful planet. The challenge is also to integrate into daily life ways to experientially and consciously connect to spiritual, universal reality. No-one and everyone must repeatedly re-engage and merge. This challenge is not easy because fourth-dimensional intellect driven onwards by third-dimensional biological drives have dominated human consciousness until now.

The sub-streams that were less intellectually endowed have been mostly overwhelmed and dissipated by generational interbreeding. Such sub-streams were closer to nature in every way, but lacked the futuristic propulsion that those who now rule your global societies have. Most such souls have had to reincarnate into unfamiliar circumstances and are unfitted to conform to prevailing dominant social norms. In a strange way this is inevitable because the original hybrid breeding programs favored the more intellectually endowed. But this was at a price and a risk. The more naturally endowed consciousness that is typical of most Indigenous peoples and of all non-human species, is also a vital part of any human being. Therefore what you have now is a broad spectrum of consciousness types co-existing, but often disharmoniously.

This has created an urgent need for higher consciousness types to lead humanity towards its potential destiny. This is only partly happening. The transition from fourth-dimensional to fifth-dimensional domination is gradual and painful. The challenge is both internally and externally to bridge across the gulf and in the process leave behind all manner of habits that are unproductive and indeed destructive.

Walking the Talk

It is not easy growing up. The ways of a child are so different from those of the adolescent and then the adult. It is essentially the same in the context of evolutional transformations. Within all metaphorical transitions there are rites of passage representing initiations into the next phase. This is how it is in theory but in practice it is somewhat more variable and problematic. What actually happens is an admixture of the preceding and future phases. You are literally in-between entities, always influenced as a push from the past and a pull from the future. The mind is intermediary and for this reason walking the talk is rarely straight-forward. The hybrid nature of humans is the genesis of the battle, both inner and outer, personal and collective. Humans are constantly involved in an inner tug of war. Walking the talk is another way of describing 'integration.'

The schism between threads in the human tapestry was realized from the outset of hybrid interbreeding. It was known there would be risks. Why then did it happen? Our intergalactic and interstellar ancestors were incapable of physical incarnation in the way humans are. The highest mammalian branch of human ancestry was little more than an advanced stone-age humanoid. The impulse was present within our interstellar hybrid branch that a planet such as yours with its developed physical creatures including quite advanced mammals had been created for an opportunity to experiment towards an aspect of Creator's vision. Human potential is the reason it happened. Human potential can only be appreciated to the extent that it is realized. The implications of this fact are profound. If the perception is limited, as it is for all who are fourth-dimensionalist, the coloration that overcovers everything is a prime determining factor in all thought and action. Walking the talk for a predominantly fourth-dimensionalist may be sincere but lacks sensitive depth and spiritual understanding. Third-dimensional non-human creatures walk their talk too but within the confines of their evolutional status. Fifth-dimensional consciousness should not be thought of as morally superior but simply of a more evolutionally advanced stage, but even then only in a particular context. The vision of Homo-spiritus, the spiritual human, is not the only dream Creator is having. Though it is the dream that humans are especially connected to, even if subconsciously.

Non-human biological species by and large have not been genetically engineered to the same extent and in the same ways as humans have. The multi-dimensionality involved in the human genetic interventions is a major difference. Humans are truly interstellar and intergalactic beings. Even the human part needs to be understood in its galactic and interstellar context. Life on your planet didn't just arrive from nowhere, nor did it simply form out of earthly natural substances, whether in ocean or on land. Everything existing in your universe is universal. Nothing living exists in a separated bubble.

Walking the talk for human beings can then refer to different status depending on the type of consciousness under consideration. The struggle between dimensions or layers of consciousness and therefore perception and understanding is what calls for integration. This is then again a complex topic and for that all the more fascinating.

Motivation

What motivates an incarnated human to do anything? Withdraw deep into yourself and ask this. What motivates you from moment to moment other than the sheer force of habit? Become aware of the range of motivations and then ask what motivations bring you joy, energy, inspiration and purpose? Or are these phenomena motivations themselves? Is there a prime motivator that sits behind all others?

Life itself or if you will, consciousness, abhors a vacuum. Nothing happens in a vacuum. There are no universes in vacuums. Hence to be a part of a universe implies movement and action. There is a motivation to move and act but to where and what? An incarnated human is a microcosm of the Supreme Being that was motivated to create the universe you co-exist in, therefore understanding is within you.

If you contemplate inwardly you will discover something. What most motivates you? You will find many competing motivations all related to desires and fears: motivations to want something or to be rid of something. A vacuum should not be confused with quietude.

Substances and Human Potential

Humans are multi-dimensional beings and this includes third dimensional biological status. In order for the various human dimensions to blend harmoniously, a conscious integration is required. This cannot happen if the entire complex multidimensionality is compromised by substances that distort and disturb coherence.

Your world is now so subjected to substances that disturb multidimensional coherence that collective consciousness is truly crippled and disempowered. Human potential is rendered vastly ineffectual, and in this sense it is the lowest common denominator that proliferates rather than a highest common denominator. This must be turned about.

Substances are chemical and psychic alterators. They act as possessors of spirit and mind. They sever the natural intimacy that could exist between dimensions and literally lock souls into imprisoned sectors. They weaken natural will and replace it with hazy powers that belong to third and fourth dimensional selfhood but without fifth-dimensional overview and guidance. They especially bring biological tendencies to the fore and in that sense are animalistic. Human potential is such that any unnatural element introduced into the complex matrix of multi-dimensional selfhood limits it. It warps potential and creates evolutional directions that are distortions of Creator's vision.

Everything is energy and either contributes towards or against potentials inherent in all living entities. These potentials are like original blueprints that guide living organisms towards optimum evolutionary outcomes. When this natural cosmic process accelerates by way of interventions such as genetic engineering, differing original blueprints become mixed and the potential for varied evolutionary directions increased, including the potential for additional power impulses towards Creator's vision. This Source-vision could be said to be the supra-vision underlying all others. It lives within all living entities to one degree or another, even in its most primitive forms, as the will to survive and fulfil essential inherent potentials.

Substances may accelerate particular potentials but at the expense of the integrated whole. Substance abuse is especially problematic when external substances become an addictive part of a soul's spiritual unfoldment. In some contexts external substances can be part of ritualistic initiations but these are traditionally within Shamanistic tribal communities and when imitated in your western modern societies, are dangerous. The desire to accelerate spiritual growth is a potent motivation but can easily lead to immature outcomes.

Spiritual immaturity, of course, expresses in multitudes of ways, but most of them have a lack of inter-dimensional and multi-dimensional integration at their core. The psychology of spiritual immaturity is once again complex and is made more so by virtue of the fact that humans are generally immature. Immaturity is a common condition but in spiritual realms its impact is especially damaging. Why is that so? Because spirituality is the way of greatest understanding, of answering the deepest questions humans are capable of asking. And yet it too has fallen often into illusion and foul play. The reasons for this essentially exist within the individual. Humans incarnate into an innocent forgetfulness. Any memory at birth is a condition of mute experience. The mind with its capacity to express in words has yet to be developed. The wondrous development of language, once underway, is channeled into societal norms that define reality. This is already so culturally conditioned that spiritual immaturity has its roots in particular cultural settings.

Birth choices are not arbitrary and therefore the environmental influences experienced by any newly incarnated human being are contextually meaningful from a karmic perspective. The predilection towards substance abuse is karmic too but past karma is not absolutely deterministic. Free will is the omnipresent gateway to potential transformation. The extent of active free will can be empowered or disempowered.

Incrementalism and Gradualism

How much freedom does an individual human being have? It varies enormously. Within this broadest of spectrums everyone can move towards optimum or minimum potential. Optimum human potential has the greatest degree of freedom. Minimum human potential has the least degree of freedom. At whatever place within the spectrum of human potential an individual is, every moment allows for another gradual, incremental movement towards greater or lesser freedom, towards or away from optimum human potential.

This is the omnipresent cutting edge of cosmic existence. The cosmic impulse is to expand but in order to do so contraction must also occur. In an evolutionary spiritual context, contraction serves expansion. The lesser is sacrificed for the greater. Such sacrifice must not be confused with integration, whereby the lesser is subsumed by the greater. Sacrifice is a sacred act. When a soul sacrifices an addiction to a substance such as alcohol, or narcotics, expansion does not include a continuation of the addictive habit. Such a sacrifice is unconditional. This is a watershed or quantum threshold. It has vast consequences for the evolutionary development of a soul.

The same principle applies to any habit that obstructs spiritual growth. It has been amply demonstrated by your neuroscientists that neural pathways in the human being are strengthened by repetition. You literally create behavioral conformity by incremental repetition. An example that is often taken for granted is action that becomes 'second nature' such as driving a car. Automatic actions related to driving, talking, or swimming, are programmed into neural memory and become easy pathways of behavior. The undoing or creating of a pathway usually occurs gradually. Use it or lose it! On the other hand a habit can cease immediately such as giving up smoking or drinking 'cold turkey.' Therefore as with all aspects of human potential there are vast degrees of difference between individuals, nonetheless when ingrained habits and especially addictions are involved, incrementalism and gradualism are the norm for most humans.

Taking a Plunge

There is a secret aspect to human potential that accounts for quantum leaps forward or backward. It is secret in so far as it goes largely unnoticed. At any moment potentially a human being can take a plunge: a choice and action that propels a soul into previously uncharted territory. Of course this potential increases beyond the limited confines of early childhood. Taking a plunge implies a soul consciously choosing to do something, as against having it done against the will. You do not realize how destiny shaping and changing this capacity is. Without it nothing much changes. Usually taking a plunge has to overcome the inertia of a particular deeply ingrained habit, the habit of remaining within the known and familiar, the habit of staying within what is felt to be a safety zone, that often needs the least energy output. No evolutionary progress has ever been made by way of inertia. Source took the plunge by exploding out of potential into actuality. Every time a soul consciously takes a plunge into new creations it replicates Source creating your universe. But there is a risk involved and consequently a seeming downside to the exercise of this potential. When a soul leaps towards a light is it a spiritual light or a train in a tunnel one is leaping into? Your much used word 'experience' is the keynote here. A soul can discern and become wise through experience. Taking a plunge need not be unwise.

What might motivate a soul to take a plunge into the unknown? Motivations can be extremely varied. What then might a mature, wise motivation and consequent plunge look like? This is an important question in order to avoid overly abstract understandings of this secret potential. A suicidal or homicidal act could be taking a plunge but we are not directing our focus towards destructive acts here but rather towards evolutionary acts of sacred value. This investigation must bring a soul to seek clarity about motivation and intention.

Our universe has purpose, and when aligned you discover your own purpose. Consciousness lights up when human purpose aligns with universal purpose. Any soul that has taken on a human embodiment can find and lose touch with itself. Self-recognition on the level of soul connects with Spirit or Source. Words only point to a transcendental experience that in reality is limitless and infinite, and yet within this field of transcendent consciousness, purpose is discovered. We then encounter the question, 'What is the Universe's purpose?' This links to the Universe's motivation too. Motivation in human terms is the inner experience driven towards fulfilling purpose. In its lower evolutional drives, motivations are essentially linked to second and third dimensional purposes: survival and biological expansion. Fourth-dimensional motivations expand into human desires, yet propelled by second and third dimensional instincts. It is with the awakening of fifth-dimensional consciousness that what was seeded by Source becomes once again realized. Source then becomes increasingly aware of itself through the vehicle of its own creation. This Self-recognition is a part of Source's and our purpose. Another part is the transformation of all dimensions into a glorious and harmonious multi-dimensional unified field of beauty. This is the great dream of the Cosmos, and secretly your own innermost soul-dream. Aspiring towards this vision of beauty and harmony is what constitutes the most evolved motivation and purpose.

The Great Threshold

Transitioning from lower dimensional into fifth-dimensional consciousness, thinking and action is easier spoken of than actualized. Indeed looked at from a fourth-dimensional perspective the transition can appear radical and monumental. And yet this evolutionary shift is also an intrinsically woven part of your purpose. Those undertaking this transition in your present time are clustered pioneers working inter-dimensionally towards and across a threshold of tremendous cosmic significance. Make no mistake; your earthly abode belongs to a cosmic experiment evolving at a magnificently refined end-part of a vast spectrum. This experiment has two major thrusts: one pro-evolutional and the other anti-evolutional. This upholds the freedom necessary for consciousness in its essential universality and purity to freely participate in a creative process. In this context you can speak of a fundamental duality. The irony of freedom allowing anti-evolutional choices and actions belongs to the unified field of supreme consciousness. Duality therefore is of a second order and yet crucial to the governing principle of your universe.

Human beings are individually as coded templates or fractals, micro-cosmically representing Source, evolving into increasingly complex but potentially more conscious entities. The dual propensities of pro and anti-evolutional forces play out throughout the entire cosmic experiment. As beings become more conscious the myriads of expressions become increasingly sophisticated. Your written and spoken languages especially become tools for both forces to extend their influences. The great threshold is symbolic of a transition occurring in your universe at this moment. At the heart of this transition is your own planetary threshold, a monumental shift in consciousness that if successful will revolutionize every aspect of your civilization. The passing over into fifth-dimensional or cosmic consciousness has always been achieved by advanced human individuals and particular groups, but the language required now must appeal to a type of fourth dimensional rationality that dwells within an industrial, technological and scientific matrix. The human brain has morphed alongside its own inventions, and the inventions themselves are by-products of consciousness coded to evolve. Therefore the great threshold is not a call to abandon materialistic and technological advances but rather to use them as aids of a spiritual consciousness that experiences all life as sacred and unified. The dual nature of consciousness must be harmonized rather than be at war with itself, if the transition is to succeed. Freedom reaches its epoch of ultimate choice for this particular experiment occurring within your solar system.

Never in the history of humanoid life on your adopted planet has there been a possibility of a mass awakening as is possible now. There have been phases where the experience and perception of great unity was prevalent, but never with a dignified intellectual and inter-dimensional wholeness as is now possible because of the evolved brain and nervous system that have developed as outgrowths of consciousness striving to fulfill its inherent potential. A mass awakening in your epoch holds a promise of never before expansions of conscious creativity, beauty, wisdom, joy and harmony. This possibility must be a mass awakening for it to enter into a paradigm of reality glimpsed by seers, prophets, artists and mystics for millennia. The vision of this Heavenly abode is coded deeply in the human soul and despite thousands of years of neglect, denial and forgetfulness burns like an eternal flame waiting for recognition and devoted adherence. It is a secret lodestar calling souls on towards Creator's dream, the dream of the Cosmos.

Every individual victory over the anti-evolutional adversary is a drop in the great collective river that leads ever closer to the tipping point, a moment when the words 'mass awakening' are describing an actual transformational event, a moment when the old ways are once and for all in spiraling disintegration and the new consciousness in unstoppable ascendency. The adversary will naturally fight to hold onto the status quo of the separatist, arrogant, narcissistic, greedy and fearful dwarf-self. The adversary is both personal and collective and belongs to the history of your universe as revealed in previous sessions. A mass awakening will be known clearly by the radically changing manifestations of your global societies. The signs and manifestations are increasing by the moment even as the adversary sharpens its defenses and aggressions. Hold to the sacred center. This is the great transformation happening before your eyes. Revelation will be your heart opening! Your heart eyes will experience revelation!

The Adversary

There is a cosmic and a shadow super-structure. The cosmic super-structure is natural and an outgrowth of sacred consciousness. The shadow super-structure is a multi-dimensional matrix that aligns with Source or deviates and is the cause of what humanity perceives as evil or dysfunctional. This deviant network is personal, interpersonal and collective. It is of paramount importance that present humanity awakens to this and gains insights into how the shadow super-structure infiltrates every aspect of their lives, and how to mitigate the effects by way of aligning with the guidance available from Source. It is this deviant structure that we refer to as the 'Adversary'. The simple and basic fact is that the deviant super-structure causes the ills that humanity and your planet suffers from. This is obviously a vastly complex subject, yet one that must be articulated and described. It challenges us more than any other topic relating to your planetary existence. Using Keith as our human interface challenges him too more than any other topic.

Acknowledge first that there is a cosmic super-structure. You refer to it as the universe. Your universe is a dynamic, evolving web of Source dreaming. It is consciousness weaving a multi-dimensional web that human consciousness is a co-participant and co-creator of, but because of the inviolable principle of freedom, individuated mind can deviate from alignment to Source: not only can, but does. It is the intention of Source and its allies that the Adversary be exposed, understood and transformed. References to the shadow super-structure are pointers to a complexity perceived by you as global civilization. In its benign state it reflects the cosmic template and paradigm, that your late theoretical physicist David Bohm named the 'implicate order'. Its manifest expression is the 'explicate order'. This is known metaphorically as 'heaven on earth.' It is such metaphors that are suggestive of the ultimate manifestation and purpose of your incarnational existence. The Adversary is anything that prevents, distorts and destroys the evolutionary process in its movement towards the fulfillment of this cosmic vision.

One way to understand the linear history of the Adversary is to realize how materialization and physicality seduce the human mind into degrees of anti-spiritual consciousness. It is difficult to comprehend that human biological physicality has changed over thousands of years, but it has. Not only has human biology 'densified' but mind has increasingly identified with body and matter. This co-opted inter-penetration, mind influencing matter and matter influencing mind, was further influenced by hybrid breeding experiments that literally altered the general evolutionary process. Your myth of the 'Tower of babel' indicates a deep memory of a time when humanoids were separated into many varied geographical groupings, each a varied hybrid group. That program involved inter-galactic humanoids from a spectrum of differing types. The idea was to establish colonies of differing hybrids and allow them to naturally evolve on your planet. The impetus behind this experiment partly belonged to a thread of the great vision of Source, to further progress spiritual consciousness within ever denser physical bodies. The risks were calculated as being worthwhile because of the potential inherent in this interventional acceleration of the great vision of Source.

One of the more potent risks was exactly that which humanity is experiencing, that of gross over-identification with matter and physicality. This process reached a new level of intensity about six hundred years ago. The age of science and reason became the new religion. When this developed into what your historians call the Industrial Age, identification with materialism began to replace nature, metaphysics, mysticism and religion. This became a new focus for some who saw in this age of industry and consumerism opportunities to amass great wealth, power and status. A new class of merchants and the beginning of modern capitalism was underway. As this developed across your world, such opportunities arose in various fields that could have established a fair and cosmically aligned structure. Economics, trade, politics, science, law, technology and corporate governance could have been manifestations of an enlightened consciousness, but a malignant worm crawled into the core of the apple. The malignant worm invades and influences the evolution of the apple on all levels of cosmic existence. It is the counter-force that pushes against sacred dreaming. It is the soul-wound at the deepest of levels within multi-dimensional existence. It can be perceived in archetypal ways as malignant principles playing through and between dimensions, but it can also be perceived microcosmically at the level of human everyday dynamics. Either way, macro or micro cosmically it is complex, but from a personal therapeutic perspective the microcosmic allows for insights that potentially can transform inner and outer reality in positive ways. In other words, in ways that orient towards the dream of Source; a dream or vision of harmony, deep understanding, love and joy.

Microcosmic Dramas

There is a profoundly deep wound within the heart of beingness that belongs to the evolutionary history of your universe and possibly beyond. This wound is the primal archetype underlying all sentient life. Essentially it is the wound of separation, a wound that was inevitable if individuality was to be seeded with any degree of inherent freedom. Human birth recapitulates this archetypal separation in a dramatic way. It is this essential separation that allows for relationship to come into existence. Without separation there can be no relationship. Therefore two opposing primal impulses begin to co-exist: the impulse to what Jung named Individuation, and the impulse of connection in relationship. These two primary impulses can potentially be in equilibrium and co-existent harmony.

The symbol of a malignant worm within the core of the apple indicates that another force enters into play that is neither harmonious nor balanced. That force which disturbs and opposes harmonious and balanced relationship between primary pairs of need is an evolutionary by product, a creative tension that propels cosmic processes into more conscious embodiments. Therefore the wound is a force that secretly insists on growth and expanded healing. The dynamic expression of the twin impulses of individuation and connection now play out in a complex spectrum of scenarios for twenty-first century

A SOUL CLUSTER COLLABORATION

humanity. Imagine walking along a street at twilight evening time. You peer into the lit up windows of individual houses. You realize that within each house a different scenario is taking place. Each house unconsciously represents a playing out of a dynamic version of the entangled twin forces of the need for individuation and the need for connection. There is no house that is untouched by this. You, walking along the street, are also a part of this. The particular circumstances of your moment to moment existence are always a part of this. This is happening within and without.

This has been occurring for millennia. Humanity is a complex web of evolving processes, both yearning for connection and solitude, for oneness and multiplicity, for universalism and personhood. Our 'up and close' encounters with others and the world at large are our own changing personal story fuelled by twin primary impulses. Life as an embodied human entails a fractal-like existence. The scenarios you encounter and help to engender are driven by archetypal forces. They are unique in the particular mix of elements but not in the greater orientation, purpose and significance. It is this bigger picture that gets obscured and hidden by the micro-details of ever-changing scenarios.

You are here to discover something amazing. Unbeknown to ordinary consciousness every encounter and scenario has a hidden intent. A microcosmic drama is a type of cryptic clue that belongs to a vast web of inter-related dramas, and they too belong to a great matrix, that has a secret mega-impulse and intent. When a particular drama is experienced as chaotic and challenging a larger context is difficult to perceive. You can get overwhelmed by the sheer complexity of details that make up your present scenario. And yet no situation is a random, unrelated, meaningless occurrence. If Keith takes his present circumstances as an example he will learn something. There are indeed a challenging set of complex circumstances but there is nothing random and meaningless about them. In the midst of complex circumstances a vital inner challenge re-emerges. Under easier circumstances the soul relaxes and more or less flows along habitual pathways. Cruise control takes over and the soul enters a type of waking dream, like driving a car without too much soul-wakefulness. But if there is a sudden traffic emergency the soul wakes and becomes alert: maybe super-alert.

What we are sharing with you is that no situation is without a great significance. You are here to awaken. Why? The reason is because you are a part of an intelligent, purposeful universe that is evolving towards an outcome. This outcome is not a fixed endpoint but a meaningful event horizon that is a part of the great vision of Source. An intelligent, loving universe and multiverse would be Source or God being self-aware through the very creation that is its embodiment. You are potentially God's eyes and heart: and when you are lost part of God is lost. Hence, your micro-dramas are complex, entangled movements seeking God. Keith can now begin to become more aware of some of the threads that make up his particular scenario.

Meditation and Mindfulness

Meditation is a complex topic to express about. Whatever is expressed about meditation is not it. And yet volumes are written about it. What is not meditation is an equally good question. And in response to both questions much can be expressed but only as pointers. Meditation is the experience behind the layers of thought and emotion that are reactive responses to the ever-changing phantasmagoria of fourth-dimensional existence.

Human beings carry the entire evolutionary history of their universe within their various energy fields. This includes the experience of Source at rest. In deep rest there is no universe. There is a way of transcending the universal drama and along with it the personal one. But if meditation is only used as transcendence it can degenerate into escapism. You are all wounded souls. Denying or escaping from the wound will backfire eventually. Christ Jesus did not deny or escape from the wound that all humanity carries. Meditation is more than transcendence. It must be transformational too.

What you refer to as 'mindfulness' is developing the capacity to be aware of what is. This includes layers of wounds that have been repressed. These wounds need acknowledging, understanding and healing, in other words, transforming.

Deconstruction and Cover Stories

From a primary evolutionary perspective an essential principle of life in your universe is survival. Built into what you refer to as the survival instinct is an automatic (read instinctive) response—towards happiness and away from pain. In this sense happiness should be understood as a natural pain-free state of existence. Humans share this dual response with all other living beings. Beings experience pain and adapt away from such circumstances. They experience happiness and veer towards those circumstances. This adaptive, evolutional survival instinct becomes far more sophisticated and complex with human beings. Over millennia humans have overlaid pain with complex strategies, mostly unconscious.

The relatively recent expanded development of the frontal cortex part of the human brain has allowed a vast potential to think and express in ways aligned with the more survival oriented middle and back parts of the brain. Source, in its evolutional march towards self-recognition within the embodied state, has inspired this development of the human brain. Now within this evolutional paradigm humans can begin to integrate multi-dimensionally or degenerate into sheer chaos. The development of the brain corresponds to the layering of consciousness. What has been constructed must be deconstructed in order for the emergence of new constructions.

If what has been constructed is non-aligned with the dream of Source then layers must be stripped away by clear insight. Mental ingenuity is such that anything can seem to be justified, even the most horrendous actions. Humans can construct cover stories to keep truth buried and denied. Cover stories are used to justify other cover stories, building up and adding to the shadow super-structure alluded to previously. To deconstruct a network of false stories can be an arduous and long undertaking, but it is the only way your humanity can truly thrive. The spiritual world is always ready to help.

Metaphorical Eruptions

In your global culture during this critical watershed phase of Earthly evolution, non-conformity to the dominating and ruling elite is often met with various forms of reprimand and punitive response. This includes the mainstream response to what is regarded as mental health. The term 'mental health' is used as a way of describing mental un-health. Psychiatry in the main is in the vanguard of scientific materialism, backed up by the pharmaceutical industry. This views 'mental health' abnormalities as illnesses residing in the brain, as organic imbalances requiring medication and other physically invasive correctives. From a fifth-dimensional perspective the standard psychiatric view is primitive, limited and lacking deep insight.

As with dreams, so-called psychotic and schizoid delusions are actually metaphorical eruptions that are generally warped time-space experiences. What is meant by 'metaphorical eruptions?' The downloading and transmitting from more universal to lower, materialized frequencies is fraught with difficulties for consciousness overly entangled in fourth-dimensional perceptions.

If you imagine a dynamic multi-dimensional and inter-dimensional hologram, with a clear center radiating out into evermore complex exterior dimensions (a holex or torus) with a primary intention to enlighten the entire network, you can begin to imagine the possible difficulties involved. Another perspective is to imagine the first dimension circling towards the fifth whereupon it completes a full circle, but with a point in the center that is dimensionless and yet the source of the movement, the Greek's notion of the 'unmoved mover.'

It could be thought that a human being is a hologram but this would be incorrect, because the center symbolizes a source that is the creator and projector of the holographic dimensions. Any creature is part hologram but essentially not so. Source is not a holographic projection. The difficulties arise because Source has initiated a universe that evolves with a degree of freedom. As holographic projective dimensions evolve through space-time, degrees of complexity increase, and in fourth-dimensional human consciousness this is perceived as physical and material diversity. The human mind has evolved 'language' that attempts to describe this diverse reality. Language is then used in a multitude of distinctly differing ways, not only use of language but perceptions, imaginations and emotions vary in type to an extent that is barely acknowledged by most of your human population. Beyond all such differences, experience itself differs widely when the spectrum of human variability is considered.

What you must remember is the purpose that evolution is imprinted to fulfill: for Source-Consciousness to become conscious of It-self within embodied entities. This implies that multi-dimensionality is recognized and integrated and that Consciousness realizes its own Divinity. When this evolutional process becomes confused, disturbed, fragmented and linguistically unsophisticated, metaphorical eruptions can easily occur. This need not be problematic. It all depends on contextual frameworks.

Without delving into the dense complexity of this topic, what is important to ask is, 'How can human consciousness move from confusion to clarity?' How can metaphoric eruptions be opportunities for creative, insightful expression rather than fragmented, chaotic, problematic experiences? A metaphorical eruption is after-all the soul's need to make sense of multi-dimensional existence, by way of pictorial, ideational, symbolic stories. In a sense all human expression is both metaphorical and metaphysical. Language itself is essentially metaphorical.

The Witness

Who is the Witness? What is your center of gravity? Who are you? Consciousness is like clear water with no ripples and no boundaries. Like a spider weaving a web from out of its own body, consciousness weaves webs of dimensions of energy and form from out of its own supreme reality. The entire multi-dimensional matrix of name and form, (Nama and rupa in Sanskrit) is a projective expression of Supreme Consciousness.

The Witness refers to a conscious recognition of Consciousness by its own faculty of self-conscious-reflection. This inner experience connects Alpha and Omega, Uroborus, the serpent of ancient occult symbolism. Meditation practice that opens portals into deep, calm, dimensionless-ness of Consciousness beyond name and form is the way to invite the Witness. The Witness can then be a Presence within the midst of changing names and forms. This is a master-key towards mastering the art of living multi-dimensionally. Then one can discover the essential qualities of Source-Consciousness beyond mere theory and belief. Imagine you are God prior to creation. You have a choice: to be or not to be. That is the question. To 'not be' means to 'not create.' To create or be at rest: 'at rest', in its fullest sense is prior to creation.

Imagine if you choose to be, to create. Only the best you are capable of will suffice. If you choose to 'not be' you are merely a Witness, but there is nothing to witness. There is only you, God, and nothing else. There is no 'part' of you, separate from you, to witness. If you choose to create even one part of yourself separate from your witnessing consciousness you will have something to witness.

What might be the motivation and intention to create, to be? Without any creation separate from Source-consciousness there is only a void. But void is not entirely empty. God must have a quality of Selfhood that would choose to create something separate. It is this quality that you name 'Love' and try to express with other essential words. Ask yourself, what is the point of creating something that you don't love? You become a loving being in self-expression. The key is to recognize yourself as Witness, able to create and express lovingly. It is your essential divine nature to do so. It is your evolutional destiny to express multi-dimensionally in love, and Witness your own creations as acts of love.

The Alchemy of Transformation

You walk through Paradise with a heavy sack of rocks tied to your back. You could untie the sack and walk free of this heavy burden but you don't. Because you don't, you don't know you are in Paradise.

The above is a simple metaphor. It needs expanding a tad. A simple yet fundamental introduction to the 'Alchemy of Transformation'.

There are three essential phases of the alchemical process: Nigredo, Solutio and Rubedo. Nigredo is essentially the conscious confrontation with all that is 'dark.' It is also known as the darkening. The darkest of the dark is the 'Death wish.' It is in truth the strongest illusion, because in ultimate reality there is no death. The death wish as an illusion is kept intact by a secondary supportive illusion, that of annihilation. Annihilation means nothingness. If a soul believes annihilation is possible, then there are no consequences beyond death. With the God-like power of freedom to choose death if I wish, there are no consequences beyond death to be concerned about. This is the fundamental, dangerous illusion within atheism. Nigredo is therefore a quantum leap into spirituality because it inspires a soul to confront the death wish, to bring it from the unconscious into the light of day.

Sigmund Freud recognized this on a lesser psychological level and named it Thanatos, the Lord of Death. I credit him for this but what I will add is that this 'force' is transdimensional and belongs to the very fabric of your galactic existence and evolution. When souls become conscious of the illusion of death as annihilation, a portal beckons. This portal is an invitation to engage in the alchemy of transformation, to step into the first phase of Nigredo. To confront the secret hiding in the darkness, that of a death wish. All wayward, destructive tendencies are expressions and manifestations of this Lord of illusions.

The ways in which you unconsciously engage in slow suicidal and homicidal actions can be brought to light, made conscious, and lead to ripeness for the second phase of the alchemy of transformation, Solutio. Solutio is the middle phase and is really the advanced process of inner transformation, essentially beyond the more 'depressive' confrontations of the long night of the soul that typifies nigredo. This phase is the conscious process of dissolving past wayward tendencies. The inner transformation can be long and drawn out or radically spontaneous. For most humans it is a long drawn out battle between progressive and regressive forces. Solutio is also known as whitening, purification of what has been putrification.

The final stage of the alchemical process is Rubedo or the 'reddening.' This is the fire of transmuting the silver of understanding into actions of gold. It is then that fifth-dimensional or spiritualized consciousness becomes an active agent in your world and Cosmos.

Merged Voices

Across the Threshhold

"What is happening in the world during 2021 and 2022, is the build up towards an evolutional threshold, a cultural volcano, a new Renaissance, and for those sensitive to the underworld, it is felt and perceived. "

Massimo

Crossing the Threshold into an Awakening of the Consciousness Soul or I Am

We can unpack the long title above. I, Massimo, have been invited to transmit through the soul and consciousness of Keith in a way that can be helpful for whoever receives these words. At this time of transmission, (December 2021) a continuation of previous discarnate transmissions is welcomed by the 'soul cluster' that we are a part of. The timing is correct.

Humanity is itself crossing over a threshold. I foresaw this while incarnated and my main book, 'The Logic Against Humanity', was an attempt to forewarn. It was simultaneously a call to the individual to awaken from a deep sleep, and a portal into understanding the collective nature of this phenomena; therefore its history or entelechy.

Keith has asked me to transmit what is especially important for those incarnated at this time of the threshold, and the title in a fashion sums it up as a simple response, but one that requires unfolding so as to be deeply understood and felt to be sufficient. The final section of the book, 'The Logic Against Humanity', is focused on the I Am or the Consciousness Soul. As a concept, I

Am is powerful, but as an immediate, self-evident, experiential insight it promises to be a foundation for a newly awakened sense of self and cosmos. It is this foundation that must be at the heart-root of any external transformation. There is no substitute or alternative for crossing the threshold from a soul sleep into an awakened consciousness, hence there is no spiritual-evolutional orientation into a vaster embodiment of the great spiritual impulses pulsing into your terrestrial environment.

This is the hour of Spirit, or Michael—the downpouring of universal forces that are useless unless received and creatively expressed. It is now the work of all who belong to soul-clusters that have divine vision in their hearts and minds. This is the nature of the Consciousness Soul or I Am. It does though require an inner crossing of a threshold and a commitment to bring a quantum shift of consciousness into active externalisations and manifestations. This is our great joint alchemical work. I am delighted to engage in an inter-dimensional collaboration with Keith and Leanne that can inspire and clarify the collective and personal nature of the threshold that humanity and the planet itself so urgently calls for.

How to Awaken the Spiritually Sleeping?

To understand how it is possible to awaken the spiritually sleeping, it is necessary to contemplate one's own inner life. But even so, this applies mainly to the individual. What about collective awakening? Is that not what Rudolf Steiner, Sri Aurobindo, Krishnamurti and many others attempted to do. Is that not what Buddha, Jesus and Mohammed intentioned? Did they succeed? Within this context how do we understand history? Is not a major consequence from these great revolutionary souls the emergence of world religions? And have world religions brought about a collective awakening of consciousness? Or is an awakened consciousness transcendent of religion? Is the nature of the Consciousness Soul, the I Am, a religious phenomena? Or is it Freedom from all conceptual categories, spiritual or otherwise?

There has never been an authentic, mass, collective awakening that transcended the particular, sectarian nomenclature of culture, geography, time and place. In other words, there has never been a universal spiritual awakening that transcended all that which wasn't universal. But there have been approximations of such a universal awakening of consciousness. The great souls who were as harbingers of universalism, who knew in their innermost being the singularity of truth and love, who were truly wise, could not transpose their awakened consciousness to others because of a cosmic and human law, that of freedom. Only in freedom can individual human beings awaken. And only when the 'hour' is right, only when the bell tolls for that individual. Until then, gradation, process, development and evolution flow like a wild river. But humanity has now evolved to a threshold that has never before been encountered. And questions regarding collective awakening have never before been as pertinent. I shall leave this as an open question for now. How is a collective awakening to happen, given that it has never happened before? Is it possible?

Soul Cluster (Group Mind)

I wish to communicate about the nature of the spiritually aligned group-mind or what Elucia has described as 'Soul Cluster'. The physics, or meta-physics pertaining to this collective psychic phenomena is of special significance at this time on your planet. I am honoured to be a part of such an ongoing experiment, an experiment that includes inter-dimensional collaborations.

There are many aspects to this topic of group-mind that are important to understand, and more than understanding, to 'know' by way of an in-turning of consciousness into its own depths. This is how an affirmative consolidation occurs of what otherwise would remain a theory or a hypothesis. An example is the statement, that a human self-image is a tiny fractal of the greater reality of who one is. Moreover, an independent and therefore, separate self is an illusion from any authentic spiritual perspective. The ordinary sense of self belongs to the most physical and cerebral level of identity. It inhabits a linear time-space mental environment that has become the dominant worldly, cultural belief. Within this environment it 'appears' that every living being is separate by virtue of their individuated bodies. Every butterfly, bird, animal and human appears separate, and indeed they all are on the physical dimension.

But beyond the physical and biological domain, there are many other dimensions of consciousness and 'self', that are increasingly less separate, until at a deeply spiritual degree, there is a merging of 'selves' into a vaster unified entity.

Group-mind operates mostly unconsciously for every human being. Especially important at your juncture of history is the participation of awakening humans into spiritually aligned group-mind collaborations. Beyond the linear space-time dimension of awareness there is a less limited and more fluid depth of consciousness. Here, a principle operates that is of a different quality, a different frequency. It is attracted to a universal reality that vibrates and oscillates in harmony with itself, like an orchestra. The principle I want to highlight here, is that thoughts and interests attract similar thoughts and interests. There is a common or aligned intention and imagination. The many individual instruments merge into a single, unified symphony.

It is this principle that now needs to be applied to Group-mind spiritual explorations and experiments. This is what I mean by the physics and metaphysics of 'Soul-cluster' or Group-mind collaboration. There is a great calling for humanity to enter into a more spiritually evolved consciousness, to usher in the Age of the Consciousness-Soul.

Immediacy

There is a timeless or eternal moment when the immediacy of consciousness activates an impulse, brings thinking, feeling and willing into alignment and crosses the threshold between ideation and manifestation. Human beings experience this unconsciously, but when consciousness is aligned with both the spiritual and worldly dimensions, such an immediacy, "the Power of Now, or Be Here Now", incarnates a cosmic impulse.

Rudolf Steiner's masterful sculpture, the Representative of Humanity, depicts the figure of Christ with one arm lofted up and the other down, simultaneously linking Heaven and Earth. This sculpture also clearly reveals the necessity to meet and transform all that would obstruct an integration between the spiritual and human dimensions. This archetypal dynamic has an evolutional entelechy, or purposeful directive that plays out in third and fourth dimensional human history. This my friends, is an outline pointing towards insights into the present worldly situation you find yourselves in the midst of.

What will bring about a collective shift in consciousness? An immediacy of impulse that has reached its moment of thinking, feeling and willing, and suddenly explodes into manifestation. Such a moment changes historical orientations for ever. Until such a moment, until such a quantum leap, a gradualism and incrementalism builds largely beneath the outer screen of externalities. What power there is in that moment a volcano erupts or an earthquake implodes. What is happening in the world during 2021 and 2022, is the build up towards an evolutional threshold, a cultural volcano, a new Renaissance, and for those sensitive to the underworld, it is felt and perceived.

I foresaw this and am now intimately engaged from the discarnate realm as are many others that belong to our soul-clusters. All the turmoil and suffering will not be in vain. My advice is, do not waste time and energy on trivialities. This is the 'Hour of Spirit'.

Aleksandr

To prevent freedom is to bring about captivity, literally to capture the spirit of freedom.

The soul who was named Aleksandr has now merged into the discussion.

The subsequent principle to survival, sacred for all human beings, is freedom. Survival is a given. Nothing else is possible without survival, without the continuation of Life. All sentient beings share in the impulse to want to survive. When a Being has evolved to the status of human, the principle of freedom is added to survival. Without freedom, the human is rendered less than truly human. Therefore, the repression and suppression of freedom is the primary adversary of human evolution. In freedom, we choose what to think, feel and do. In freedom, we learn from experience.

The entire history of humanity can be perceived as a complex process of two forces: freedom and enslavement. These two forces continue to intereweave both within the individual and in society. Naturally, there is need to balance freedom with discipline and boundaries, but in freedom. To prevent freedom is to bring about captivity, literally to capture the spirit of freedom. To coerce the spirit of freedom, to subjugate it by way of threat or punishment, or to weaken it by promise of reward, is to violate the second most important principle of human existence.

The third most important principle for the human being, following survival and freedom, is choice. Choice involves the 'will'. Free will is the faculty within consciousness to choose what to think, feel and do. It implies 'autonomy'. To prevent human autonomy is to attempt to replace it with automatism. It reduces the human being to a robotic, unfree slave. This principle of enslavement is what Rudolf Steiner referred to as the force of Ahriman.

Without freedom there cannot be love and truth. Love and truth cannot be forced. They must be taken up within consciousness in freedom. The immediacy of cognising freedom is itself an inner awakening to its own reality. It invites true friendship. It liberates consciousness from all that imprisons it. It then acts as a foundation for an emerging external culture truly worthy of human potential, the evolving into fifth dimensionality Homo-spiritus.

Moral Choices

The idea of 'choice' belongs to a much misunderstood principle, that of morality. What does a moral choice made in freedom look like? Is there a universal morality that transcends differences in culture? The answer is yes. The archetype is everywhere about us. The cosmos works beautifully. And it is not controlled by human beings. Galaxies function on a macro scale compared to our solar system and planet, but all exhibit a natural ordering that represents the principle of morality. In other words, morality is a principle that 'holds things together.' It allows disparate elements to co-exist; it sustains itself as an integral whole system. Morality is not about the individual part, but rather the whole. It is holistic. This is the archetypal model of morality that cosmic and earthly nature presents to us: a 'holex' or 'gestalt' that moves us to consider a bigger picture than any particular consideration.

This is the portal into universal morality, intrinsic to the human soul, because humanity is part of the living cosmos. Therefore, making moral choices is a natural component of being human. But because of the principle of freedom, a moral choice must be freely chosen. The human condition is more complex than a simple choice between moral and immoral possibilities. The workings of consciousness are far too complex within linear space-time, but underneath the matrix of karmic tendencies and multifarious beliefs, there is universal clarity, a singularity of Gnosis, an I Am or Consciousness-Soul, that equates fully with the principle of morality. It is within our human-spiritual nature to cognise with this inner and outer foundation and align our human choices accordingly.

From a human incarnate perspective universal morality is as looking through a telescope out into the cosmos. From a discarnate perspective it is as if looking through a microscope into the world of particles. Either way can offer a glimpse into universal harmony and morality.

Before investigating the complexities that surround universal morality within the human sphere, can there be a personal and collective awakening to such a foundational truth in its self-evident essence? Can Creator or God Consciousness recognise itself in a meditative immediacy of awakened experiential awareness? Can the dominant cerebral cortex quieten and soften, allowing a sudden epiphany of deeper awakening to emerge? These transmissions are not intended to be New Age esoteric intellectual entertainment. They are at the very least an invitation to contemplate beyond ordinary ways of thinking. You are a sovereign autonomous soul that belongs to a universal family of other sentient souls. Among this vast family there are especially meaningful connections. This is your more intimate soul family or soul-cluster. The I Am belongs both to yourself and merges with those who you collaborate with to become 'We Are'. It is this We-ness that beckons us towards an evolutional leap into fifth dimensional global culture, but only as a movement of freedom, morality and awakened consciousness.

Humanity stands on a threshold between two paradigms. They are entangled, but can unravel into a golden age, or collapse into an unspiritual mechanical bio-techno-materialism. It is truly up to us individually and collectively. We are responsible for the choices made and their consequences. We (our merged soul cluster) will investigate the nature of the entrapment humanity is caught within and the possible movements beyond entrapment into a free moral global culture. This is an ongoing process of collaborative incarnate and discarnate researches into a cosmic and human experimental challenge. It is why we are 'here'. It is the reason for Being.

Blessings.

Entrapment

By 'entrapment' we mean being trapped in grids, systems, ideologies, etc that deviate from or are unaligned with cosmic nature or the implicate order. The 'Ground Zero' of cosmic and earthly nature is its fundamental reality, free of particular interpretations and secondary data.

Human thinking entered into this evolutionary unfoldment at some point. Human thinking then crossed a threshold into degrees of free will and hence thinking itself became a force that shaped the external environment. Ancient stories mythologise this threshold-crossing. Humankind could now rise beyond nature, and thinking became super-nature that subsumed nature in its vaster consciousness of freedom. This is Godhead's experiment: the permission for humankind to think for themselves. It is here, at the threshold between nature and super-nature, that entrapment has its genesis.

Pause for a moment and contemplate what has just been transmitted. Because this threshold yet exists within the human soul. Can you perceive that entrapment belongs to thinking? And as we shall pursue in 'Beyond Entrapment', moving beyond entrapment likewise belongs to the potential within thinking.

Thinking does something that goes generally unnoticed.

It creates layers of images, ideations and beliefs that are superimpositions atop of 'what actually is'. Thinking in this context cannot be separated from language. We think linguistically. We observe an object and attach language to it. And we do the same when we look within ourselves. Language becomes the filter between what is, and a description of what is. Thinking uses language to create meaning within the actual reality of living experience.

But there are other forces at play. What forces are as impulses that influence thinking? What forces are inspirations for thinking? What forces entrap human souls in grids that do not further natural evolution? Rudolf Steiner named some of these forces as Christ, Lucifer and Ahriman. Goethe had his Mephistopheles. Forces in this context signify whatever is nonaligned and disruptive to nature and super-nature in their pure being.

This is an introduction to the topic of entrapment. It is not a topic unrelated to what is happening in 2021/2022 in Australia and the world. What is happening at this time is a fractal of a larger story which is also a fractal of a larger story. The essential script belongs to a historical archetype. Can we strip this to its archetypal bones? Once upon a time, human consciousness was naturally aligned with the cosmos. A shamanistic harmony prevailed upon the earth and among all living beings. All was merged in a respectful and sensitive relationship. And then ego emerged. Ego is the I-Consciousness, separated from the all. This development led to a radical shift in the way many humans perceived and thought about themselves and others. Humans could now think for themselves beyond the confines of nature (instinct). This was the beginning of a new direction in human evolution. It brought about a powerful sense of autonomy and individuality. It shifted human communities away from tribalism and towards transactionism, a way of relating to others with self-interest dominating. What was and still is a major factor relating to this shift in human consciousness, is the use of language. An element crept in that has had a monumental influence on language, and consequently, every part of human society. To state it simply(at this moment), language became a tool for entrapping ourselves and each other in complex webs of unspiritual egoism. Language became a way of expanding self interest at the expense of the 'common good'. The older 'tribal' and Shamanistic consciousness became overwhelmed by various forms of modern sectarianism. Language adapted itself to a change in consciousness. This occurred over vast stretches of time and was complicated by virtue of the different root races inhabiting the planet. But the main point is to understand how language shapes our world view,our reality, in fact everything we think, and consequently, we do.

Why does the human faculty of thinking entrap us? After all, it doesn't have to. It is essentially because of the spiritual, God-given principle of freedom, mythologised by Adam and Eve. Eating the apple initiated a new entry-point, the crossing of a new threshold, into the evolutionary saga of humanity. In short, Homo-Sapiens are now responsible for what they think and the consequences thereof. One could describe the quantum shift from instinct to free-will as the crossing of the threshold into the age of imagination. Thinking can imagine beyond the confines of survival instincts. Observe nature meditatively, and you can gain insight into the instinctual realm that allows for the continuation of life. Observe birds. They know what to do. They don't need imagination. They know how to survive. Trees know too. So do galaxies. And then comes an awesome quantum leap into human imagination. At some point humans could imagine possibilities beyond the instinctual-survivalist realm. They imagined domesticating animals. They imagined village life, agricultural practices and commerce. They invented language. There was no limit to what a human being could potentially imagine.

It is at this threshold in human evolution that a curious feature emerges, that of morality: the inner discernment that knows right from wrong. Inwardly knowing what was right and wrong was an extension from an earlier instinctual realm, an extension into consciousness and into thinking. This evolved into language. Language reflected the inner thinking. And thinking was unfettered from instincts to freedom. Thinking was released from nature and survival, and could imagine in abstract ways. This is the foundational legacy of our present human condition, both individually and collectively.

The change was one that shifted consciousness into an awareness of itself. It was the beginning of human thinking, rather than instinctual nature, being the dominant force, a force that would henceforth shape human culture, the foundation upon which humanity becomes entrapped in its own creations, and as we shall explore, within which it can move beyond entrapment.

How is it possible for a human being to exist in heaven and hell simultaneously? The fact is the vast majority of humanity do so. We (humanity) create both heavenly and hellish environments and circumstances. We freely entrap ourselves and each other. The entire manifestation of human civilisation belongs to the capacity for free-will and autonomous, individuated thinking.

Humanity is a genetic experiment par-excellence, a merging of two vastly different paradigms: nature and super-nature, instinct and ego-consciousness. Yet there is a price to pay for this grand experiment. At the dawn of the human experiment on Gaia, Beings from elsewhere visited and genetically mixed themselves with the local inhabitants. The visitors were God-like compared with the natives. In the Old Testament, Moses asks the Force that has manifested as the Burning Bush and a super-natural voice transmitting the Ten Commandments, "Who should I say you are?" The voice answers, "Say I Am That I Am." This could be likewise understood as, 'I Know That I Know'. It is this Self-knowing or Gnosis that distinguishes human from pre or non human. By genetically mixing these two primal elements, essentially consciousness and sub-consciousness, super-nature and nature, a type of hybrid is engendered, and humanity is such a hybrid in many different streams of genetic mixing. The inter-breeding experiments were between the Gaian (Earthly) natives and a confederation of inter-galactic beings, hence a geographical diversity was instituted that became the origin of the different human 'racial' types. Within this scenario the most important aspect is what can be termed 'cosmic morality'. The most astounding feature of the universe is that it works. In its mind boggling complexity, it allows for life to thrive and evolve. This is morality. The word 'moral' can be broken up into M-oral. As if once the 'word' has been spoken (oral), a frequency, a wave (M) brings a new dimension into play. The invisible becomes visible. The sound becomes manifest. The Divine becomes embodied. Consciousness becomes self-knowing. The Being recognises itself in its own mirror image. Everything external becomes aligned with the internal. The 'implicate order' is cognised in its 'explicate' manifestation. The alignment is morality. Non-alignment is immorality or a-morality, meaning lacking morality. We can explore this as we proceed.

Humanity carries its own vast history within its genome and its deep consciousness. The entire history of the many ways we entrap ourselves and each other is encoded within our psyches. The diverse genetic components within our embodied history are secondary to the power of the consciousness-soul, striving towards self-knowing as a plant seeks the sun and the rain. In the re-cognising of morality there can be no coercion of another that violates the principle of freedom. To violate this principle of freedom is to step out of morality; to miss the mark, to transgress. At this threshold we stand and can ask, how can we individually and collectively transform beyond entrapment? The I Am Consciousness-Soul is both what entraps and can evolve beyond entrapment. It must first cognise its central role. In the work with and by Massimo, especial consideration was given to the many ways that the I Am entraps itself. No matter how clever the logic becomes that justifies untruth, the I Am sits behind the curtain awaiting the moment of self-recognition. If the curtain itself has become more like a complex matrix, so be it, but from the perspective of the I Am, there is only one truth, and it is unchanging in its essential nature. It is I Am That I Am. It is moral. It is aligned. It is kind. And yet for most human beings in this dystopian era, a transition from entrapment to beyond entrapment is fraught with difficult challenges. What will empower souls to cross the threshold into freedom? What will reorient humanity towards a global morality? What needs to happen?

Beyond Entrapment

It is fundamentally simple. YOU are the ruler of both ignorance and knowledge. You are the I Am Consciousness Soul shining through every element that is created. You are the source of every thought, every feeling and every action. Therefore, you are transcendent (beyond) of every religion, philosophy and ideation. If YOU can cognise this even for a moment, the insight can emerge that it must be possible to totally move beyond the entrapments of false identification. But such a moment would be only the beginning, much like observing a tip of an iceberg.

And then...and then it must become an intentional practice. Ground zero must be re-cognised again and again. Gradually inner consciousness becomes grounded in its own freedom. Incrementally the entrapments dissolve, weaken, subside, and fall away. Great spiritual literature and art offer bridges that span across the great divide, the threshold that divides suffering from bliss, anxiety from calm abiding. The struggling ego responds, 'If only it was that simple or easy'. Sure, but it is all of one's own making. Know thyself is indeed the portal into Homo-spiritus. It is not simple only because we have complicated it. It is not easy only because we have made it difficult. And if truth be told, the ego has become addicted to much of what is complicated and difficult. Beyond entrapments is not only possible but the reason why we are alive. The reason to bake a cake is not for it to be removed from the oven half-baked. Nor are we meant to only study the recipe book. So these indications regarding 'beyond entrapments' can only approach the actual experience of freedom from different angles, hinting at ways to take the journey. The horse once taken to the sparkling waters of the oasis must choose to drink. Nonetheless, some advice can be added to the world's storehouse of spiritual insights or dharma. And there are indeed many, many teachers, artists, books, films, etc, who are worthy light-bringers to darkened places. The key element is your own sovereign, spiritual consciousness.

Embodiment is a dance between two very different partners: infinite and finite, consciousness and thinking, being and becoming, awake and asleep. The dance is between two archetypal forces that constitute the human being. The problem herein is one of imbalance. The identification with finite, thinking, becoming and whatever entices the soul into a virtual coma is the obstacle, that which causes and maintains the unbalance. And yet, in any moment of immediacy, the Consciousness-Soul can remember itself as sovereign ruler. The dance can then be led by spirit, by the infinite, in freedom and with a moral heart. The two inner dance partners can synchronise beautifully, poetically, gracefully. When this occurs within individuals, among those who likewise are discovering sacred balance, soul clusters can emerge naturally and unforced. This is the way forward into a transformed culture of which seers and spiritual poets have glimpsed within their own meditative visions.

We carry the divine seeds within our souls. There is an inner and outer paradise awaiting on the other side of the great river. We are on the way. Those of us who choose freedom over enslavement, loving kindness over narcissism, truth over illusion.

Together we shall cross over the threshold, live in harmony and peace, and continue to creatively engender ways to help others cross over too. For this is our mission, chosen long ago. And after eons of falling into every type of entrapment, we gradually awaken as if from a long, long dream, and discover those souls who yearn for the new land, as we do. Together we move in the assured knowledge of success, knowing that divine love and truth must conquer all, transform all.

Learning patience as we orient towards the place beyond entrapments, beyond illusions, a vast strength enters as a spiritual wind. For it is known beyond all doubt, that this is our birthright: to know who we really are, to be who we really are, to embody the divine. In the midst of all that changes, the consciousness-soul remembers itself as the immortal living being. We pass through each incarnation as guests in a strange land. We emerge again and again, become somewhat lost in the scenery, and return at the appointed hour to our discarnate home. Such is the metamorphosis. But as with babies, insects, fish, birds and animals, the living essence knows how to be. And yet the soul intuits that there is more. Beyond the entrapments that our karmic tendencies lead us into, heaven on earth awaits. That heaven, that explicit order mirroring cosmic love and wisdom, that manifestation of embodying the divine, is as close as our own sovereign autonomy, our universal God-self. The amazing thing is that the actual experience that such words point towards is omnipresently here, here and now. Drop the illusion and clear vision emerges. We are here to awaken each other.

The modern trap is now manifesting all around us as biological and technological interventions. We can blame 'them' or 'it' but the real trap, as always, is within our own minds and emotions. The external agencies that are used to infiltrate us are powerless if the soul is awake and strong in its conviction. What is happening is actually an exposure. The Emperor is gradually being stripped of his clothes, even if most are still not noticing. The Emperor is a cabal made up of very powerful people from many walks of life, corporate, media, political, technological, banking, military, transport, pharmaceutical, medical, mining, agriculture, royalty, religious and others. The head of the beast is media. Global mainstream media broadcasts to the majority of the world's population its version of reality. All of the institutions named above and others are not so much conspiring but rather entwined with each other and have a common orientation. Since the so-called industrial revolution, roughly the mid 1700's, the world became dominated by commercial interests. Even before, this colonisation by countries such as Great Britain, France, Holland, Spain, Portugal and others increasingly opened up the world as a market place. And factories that became the means for mass production created the capitalistic world that now dominates global culture. This spawned infrastructures, multinational organisations, grids of every type, and in general became the new normal. This is the external manifestation of inner forces. What are those inner forces? In other words, what motivates, directs and shapes the external matrix? Human imagination, once enabled to freely function however it chooses, becomes a force for great good or evil. Whether imagination is aligned or non-aligned with morality becomes a vital question. The principle of imagination and its relationship with morality has a historicity that takes us back into the mists of early human development. But I wish to highlight an important feature powerfully relevant to the present era.

The question that wannabe totalitarians pondered for centuries is, 'How do I gain and maximise control over others?' The invention of the printing press together with higher levels of literacy among the 'lower classes' allowed for a greater reach into people's minds. People everywhere, at least in the more developed nations, were to be observed with their faces buried in newspapers. This provided a massive opportunity to influence the general population. Capitalism now had a powerful advertising outlet. But this new public phenomenon of the daily newspaper became a tool for every type of political and social propaganda, bias and agenda. The news itself became tainted with whatever the owners and their editors selectively chose to appear in print. We can only intuit the degree of influence that this communication media had on the masses. What a leap forward then it was when radio became a popular feature in people's homes. Now the human voice with its tones could be merged with the information being broadcast. And the human voice can be trained to sound warm, trustworthy and authoritative. Then there was the cinema followed in the 1950's by television. And now we have the internet and social media. All these communication technologies exponentially increased the power to influence the world's population. And didn't the cabal know this. Hence the imaginative idea about taking control of the world's mainstream media as the way to have control over future humanity and the planet itself has become the underlying motivation for various related agendas to shape the future according to a specific master-plan: a vision of the future.

A problem is, no one asked me for my input. In fact, I wasn't even told it was happening. Mainstream media became entrapped into the cabal's grids and machinations, but fortunately I discovered other off-grid sources of information. I now stand firmly outside the manipulated mainstream matrix, looking in. The details of human entrapment are complex almost beyond comprehension. Many others have explored and shared parts of this complexity. But one principle is of utmost importance. If we are to move beyond entrapment in our thinking, in our very souls, then firstly we must see clearly the essential nature of entrapped thinking.

Entrapped thinking cannot free itself. But who You really are is not entrapped. The wild bird trapped in a cage is not really trapped. Open the cage door and it will fly away. On the level of entrapped thinking we can speak of entrapment, but such thinking is as a foreign substance that doesn't belong to human consciousness in its sacred nature. In other words, entrapment is an evolutionary superimposition.

A further development into a transformed future would naturally be to move beyond entrapped thinking. Entrapped thinking has become materialised and manifested into a cultural phenomena. But it can be seen for what it is. I remember my son at a very early age, watching a TV advertisement and remarking, 'They are not telling the truth. They are just trying to make us buy it'. Great insight. It's not rocket science. What we are generally told across the world's mainstream media is not the truth. It has now become more true than ever before. The cabal knew that controlling media would be tantamount to controlling humanity, and controlling humanity is their aim. The television set is known as the 'idiot box' for a reason. Television has largely betrayed its greater potential, because it is human thinking, human imagination and vitally, human morality, or lack of, that sits behind all manifestation. Without moral thinking, other degenerate forces enter into the psyche; into the soul. And morality in its spiritual realm aligns with honesty, courage, transparency, kindness, compassion and love. It is immoral to lie, be cowardly, deceive, be unkind and hateful. Crossing the great river beyond entrapment demands a moral renaissance, not just a few but on a mass scale. It demands a recalibration of human thinking and human culture. Can this take place?

We now come to the single most important message regarding crossing the river of transformed being and thinking: crossing over the threshold between being entrapped and liberation. It is the sovereign I Am, the Consciousness-Soul, autonomous and yet aligned with cosmic morality, that on awakening to itself cognisently, can inspire an immediate shift of consciousness. It is not knowing thyself that is the ultimate obstacle to being able to freely choose to think and live morally. In knowing thyself a further step is needed. 'I know therefore I make the right choice.' And when the spiritual neophyte (apprentice) falls, there is the always the redemptive return. This is the message: know thyself and strengthen the intention to think and live morally.

Descartes coined the dictum 'I think, therefore I am.' This is only partly true. The other part is 'I Am, therefore I think,' for they belong together. The I Am, Consciousness-Soul, thinks, and therefore cognises through thought and language, its own being. To only cognise thought as the evidence of being is to avoid the direct experience of being. Thinking only proves that being (I Am) thinks. This is not some abstract philosophical or linguistic exercise. The I Am is Consciousness in its infinite timelessness, and is the foundation of who 'we' are. It is therefore the I Am that thinks itself into entrapments and can at any moment move beyond entrapments. These words point to the exit but the experience is non-transferable. It is solely within the subjective inner realm. Freedom is knowing experientially who we are.

Afterword

Awakening,

Like a magic wand, or a sacred kiss,

Is omnipresently available.

You are thinker,

Not that which is thought,

Doer,

Not that which is done.

You are consciousness,

Infinite and free.

Take hold:

Hold the line!

My Own Freedom Story

The soul strives to free itself from entrapments in many ways during an incarnate life-span. This happens often without reflection and therefore without insight. And yet each time a person moves out of entrapment and into freedom, even though it only be related to a specific situation or event, it belongs to a core aspect of personal development. Understanding this invites reflection on personal 'freedom stories' that are perceived as being significant parts of one's biography. Freeing oneself from entrapments can either be initiated by one's own effort and choice, or be brought about by external circumstances. I finished the shambles of English public schooling a few months after my fifteenth birthday. It was an externally brought about move out of a tortuous entrapment.

Four years later I suddenly made a decision that not only freed me from another entrapment, but would have a major influence on the rest of my life. On this occasion it was my subjective choice that freed me. I had become entrapped in an apprenticeship that didn't belong to my greater destiny. The nature of the entrapment wasn't due to Alan, my employer. He was a good man. It wasn't due to the type of work. It simply wasn't aligned with who I really was. It was seemingly a work day like all those over four years that preceded it. The only thing that was out of the ordinary is that Alan was not present. He had begun his annual holiday, leaving Colin, the foreman in charge of the ongoing operations. There were three other apprentices, Colin, Gerard (who rented a space) and myself. It was early afternoon. After four years of fulfilling my expected duty, I suddenly stood up and said to Colin, "I've had enough. I'm going to leave." Colin responded, "What do you mean? Don't you feel well? Do you want to leave early today?" I took a deep breath. "No, I mean I've had enough of this job. I need to leave and do something else with my life". Colin tried to dissuade me for a while and then surrendered to what must have appeared definite as much as radical. Gerard asked me, "What will you do?" I hadn't given that a thought, and yet a part of me answered, " I'll buy a back-pack and travel around Europe." And I left the workplace and not long after travelled around Europe.

Why did I do this? Alan was a good employer. I was being trained by one of London's best jewellers. I only had a little over a year left of my apprenticeship. But another destiny called me. Alan probably intuited this from early on. It wasn't a mistake. I learnt important lessons during those four years. But in regards to my greater destiny I was entrapped. My soul knew it. And my answer to Gerard's question was my soul knowing what it needed to do. I needed to learn to trust my self, my soul; the voice within that yearns for freedom. Not aimless freedom but to be free to search for one's true destiny. I walked out of an entrapment into the unknown. In doing so, I inwardly knew or sensed that I had nothing to fear. The way that my nineteen year old self could express it at the time was,

"I'm needing to find myself", and that was correct in a very real sense. This was a step beyond entrapment, certainly not the only such threshold I've crossed, but a most significant one.

In retrospect I can glimpse how powerfully that step beyond entrapment has been. I learnt to trust life and myself. I learnt to trust in spirit before I had named it such. It has served ever since as an archetypal story of freedom within my own biography.

"A cabal is a leadership group that determines what and how everything should be."

Conversations with the Cabal

A fragment, July 2021: Held between Keith, a leading person of the Cabal and a transcarnate representative of the galactic and intergalactic Federation. These conversations continued up until Keith's crossing the threshhold in February 2022.

Cabal: We have been aware of a problem confronting humanity and the planet for at least eighty years.

Keith: How did this 'problem' become realised? What is the problem in a nutshell?

Cabal: in the aftermath of the First World War, it was realised that even with the huge loss of life that occurred during the war years, the human population was growing. Within the new 'science' of Sociology, population became a topic of serious academic attention. In a nutshell, it was realised that there is a finite limit for a sustainable future for humanity in terms of population numbers. It was realised that the human population had always increased throughout recorded history, and that despite famines, epidemics and wars, an increasing exponential growth was creating a massive inbalance and threat.

Keith: So who was involved in trying to solve this imbalance and threat?

Cabal: Well, in order to understand that we need to back up.

You need to understand what the cabal is: who we are. There has always been a cabal. A cabal is a leadership group that determines what and how everything should be.

Galactic Federation: From our perspective the entire cosmos is inhabited and evolved by a cabal, that is caballah in its purest symbolism.

Cabal: And here on the earth-human plane this cabal is a replicative attempt to control human and planetary evolution, and prevent it from destroying itself. Therefore, following the Great War, a new attempt at global collaboration was instituted whose aim was partly to prevent future global conflicts but also to secretly confront the realisation of the need to break down old ways of thinking. These old ways of thinking had created great advances but also set in motion an orientation that was destroying civilisation.

Keith: How?

Cabal: From earliest recorded times a hierarchy existed here on planet earth. In its primitive forms it followed the laws of nature as with non-human creatures. With the advent of human beings, many of the hierarchical structures began to become perverted. The rulership of royalty and religion both set the pattern of the few ruling the many. In many ways this pattern has continued to the present times, but has now evolved to a critical threshold.

Federation: This is an archetypal principle. That of leadership. It exists throughout your cosmos. There are councils of such leaders within your galaxy, inter-galactically and within the multiverse.

It replicates on your planet too but for human beings it has been long perverted.

Keith: So after the Great War something new came into being?

Cabal: Never had there been a global event of such death and destruction as the Great War. The real beginning of globalism began in 1914, except it was a global hierachy that split the world into two parts. The League of Nations was formed uncomfortably alongside the Versailles Treaty. A rift between two power blocs was created. It led in its way to the Second World War. This was an example of the same adversarial thinking that had led to the Great War in the first place. Secrecy, intrigue, nationalistic hubris and petty self-interest dominated. If something new came into being it was an early realisation that humanity was moving in a disastrous direction, but this was not really deeply perceived until the end of the Second World War. There were individuals who understood this situation better than most. Rudolf Steiner was one. His 'Three-fold social order' was an attempt to create a new societal foundation. But the cabal that I am a part of was unfortunately resistant to this new vision. Most of the members of the cabal that was formed in the aftermath of the Second World War, were and still are stuck in old forms of thinking. They still identify with their 'group', which is perceived as an elite seperate from the rest of humanity.

Keith: Goethe had seen in French Napoleonic nationalism and a unified Germany formed from many states as a response, the winds of future catastrophes.

Galactic Federation: All these historical events were corrupted and degenerate examples of the failure of human thinking to replicate the unified diversity of higher levels of consciousness and the cosmos itself. As the cosmos evolved through dispersions into greater and greater materiality and physicality: the alchemical plasma of energy emanating from Source or Godhead cooling and solidifying, so consciousness itself became identified with particulars and away from the whole. Consciousness in order to evolve towards embodied beings such as humanoids and human-beings, beings that could think independently, a sense of seperateneness and apartness occurred. Tribal societies were early examples of group identity. This dispersion into diversity is a major feature of your cosmos, and especially of your galaxy and even more your solar system.

Cabal: The Cabal is made up of those who have immense wealth and hence are accustomed to living in great privilege. This has been true for me too, and as the contact chosen to communicate with you (Keith), I shall reveal to you why we have to do what we are doing.

Keith: I accept that as long as I can freely ask questions and challenge what you are sharing with me.

Cabal: A solution had to be found for exponential population growth. Not that it was perceived as the only urgent issue to be dealt with. In fact, it was tied into many other areas that were also brought to the table: such as, climate change, pollution, environment, economy, poverty, child trafficking and more. Indeed, it was perceived that capitalism in its present form was outdated and required deep change.

Keith: And wasn't it also realised that the politics of the left and right hid a singular power that used both for their purposes?

Cabal: Absolutely. The Cabal is that singular entity. It is made up at the highest level of individuals that transcend the political divide. We are in effect trans-political and therefore require all sides of politics to fall under our command.

Keith: Isn't the Cabal then a new form of trans-political totalitarianism?

Cabal: You can think of it in that way, but do you not accept that leadership is necessary?

Keith: I do accept that leadership is necessary, but there are two questions that emerge here: what type of leadership and what of the sovereignty of the individual: of the right of the individual to lead his or her own life?

Cabal: It was clear that Fascism and Communism both failed to tackle many urgent problems facing humanity: that leadership had failed to deliver. But that does not amount to abandoning leadership altogether. The Cabal is a new type of leadership. It's concern is with creating a new type of future: one that is sustainable. In other words, livable. To that effect we established new committees whose focus was on changing the old structures of the world. The Cold War was still an old form of adversarial thinking. During the social upheavals of the 1960's, new types of thinking were being brought to bear.

The Cabal in its modern form became established, hidden behind a screen of secrecy.

Galactic Federation: Members of the Galactic and Intergalactic Federations had some interventional influence throughout these years. When the atom bombs were dropped on Japan, an alert was sent out that alarmed us. A new wave of energy was released into the cosmos that threatened the sacred experiment that your planet is, and also the future possibilities of the mostly hidden inter-relationship with other humanoids and cosmic life in general. Your Cabal had to realise that humans were not alone in their universe.

Cabal: There was and is an interventional influence within this unfoldment. The hand of greater powers is present but only as an influence, not as a controlling authority. The human Cabal is free to make its own decisions. So to move forward in time. Plans for future change were being discussed at the highest levels, but increasingly it was among those who wielded the most influence. With a few exceptions that was not the politicians of the world, who obeyed orders or were removed in one way or another.

Galactic Federation: Do you begin to sense how complex this is. The Holex is a multi-dimensional quantum field, that belongs to an even vaster multiverse beyond ordinary human comprehension. There is a divine order that pulses throughout and orders everything so that it sustains, survives and evolves. What one of your most brilliant scientists realised is that there is 'an implicate order' and consciousness within human beings mostly unconsciously strives to replicate this explicately.

Your Christian symbolism of the 'Second coming of Christ' indicates that a time will come when a mass human awakening will occur, and the implicate order will be experienced as the sacred template that humanity is intended to explicate or externalise. The unholy alliance will be replaced by a Holy Alliance.

www.ingramcontent.com/pod-product-compliance
Lightning Source LLC
Chambersburg PA
CBHW031422290426
44110CB00011B/491